Madam & Eve's
South African
Survival
Handbook

By Gus Silber
with Madam & Eve characters
by S. Francis & Rico

Published in 2001 in southern Africa by
Rapid Phase (Pty) Ltd
1 Bompas Square
9 Bompas Road
Dunkeld West 2196
Johannesburg

©  RAPID PHASE (PTY) LTD 2001

ISBN 0-620-27930-3

Design & DTP by Creative Communication Alliance
Reproduction by B1 Bureau, Johannesburg, RSA
Printed by Universal Printers

Acknowledgments

The following people gave freely and willingly of their time and expertise in assisting with research into a wide variety of survival issues. Many thanks to:

Superintendent M.M. Adams, Inspector U.S. Engelbrecht, Sergeant R. Human and Superintendent C. Wilkin of the South African Police Services.

Jeremy Cliff, Executive Officer of the Research Office, Natal Sharks Board.

Chris Daphne, Game Ranger, Mala-Mala.

Mandy Momberg, Game Ranger, Pilanesberg.

Basil Mann, anti-hijacking consultant.

Dr. Peter Felderbauer, medical practitioner.

Andrew Friedemann of Wild Ways Mountaineering.

Norma Jones of Hartebeespoort Snake Park.

Mark Kopman of Glass-Arenson Insurance.

Alex Larenty and Ian Melass of the Lion Park, Lanseria, Gauteng.

Paul Marais, river guide and explorer.

Gavin Fleming, environmentalist.

Chris Kirchhoff, explorer.

David Evans, kayaker.

Jeanette Schoultz, self-defense consultant.

Rob Thomas of the Mountain Club of South Africa.

Adrian Vroom, commercial pilot.

Jacques Grobbelaar of the Civil Aviation Authority.

Dries Wehmeyer, Aviation Safety Manager, SAA.

Eddy Burgstaller of E&R Dog Training Center.

Martinique van der Westhuizen of the SA Dog Training Centre.

Jeffrey Davis of Global Special Events.

Bruce Dell of Wilderness Leadership School.

Gary Clackworthy of BMW Advanced Driving School.

Chris Challis of the AXXON Animal Handling Company.

Caroline Smith of Media Magic Public Relations and Event Management.

Johan van der Walt of Roosevelt Park Fire Station.

The CSIR.

The Red Cross.

The South African Weather Bureau.

FOREWORD

A message from Discovery

Discovery's purpose is to make people healthier, and to enhance and protect their lifestyles. That's one reason why we created the Vitality programme, which encourages our Discovery members to take better care of themselves, and rewards them when they do.

Madam & Eve's South African Survival Handbook is packed with advice about what to do when the going gets tough. Although you would have to be very unlucky to get embroiled in some of the situations described in this book, the theme of trying to prevent disasters before they happen is in keeping with Discovery's core philosophy.

We hope this book will encourage all South Africans to think ahead and be prepared.

Madam & Eve have become icons in South Africa, and we are very pleased to present a book that will not only raise a smile, but might also help South Africans from all walks of life keep out of harm's way.

Enjoy the read.

Neville Koopowitz

Marketing Director: Discovery

Contents

INTRODUCTION

FOREWORD
IS FOREARMED

As nine out of 10 survival experts will be happy to tell you (the 10th having unfortunately failed to follow his own advice), the best way to survive a life-threatening situation, whether in the suburbs, the city, or the Great Outdoors, is not to get into it in the first place.

DON'T get out of your car to take a close-up picture of a sleeping lion.

DON'T walk down a dark alley at midnight with your wallet sticking out of your back pocket.

DON'T leave a pan of oil burning on the stove while you watch the latest episode of Survivor in the lounge.

Then again, humans are a curious species in more ways than one. We are driven to test the furthest limits of endurance; we are secretly attracted by the sudden threat of danger; we deliberately venture into territories, or place ourselves in positions, where our very lives are at stake.

And all this, only while driving to work in the morning. (Remember: DON'T use both hands to signal at fellow drivers while talking on your hands-free phone).

Try as you might, therefore, to avoid getting into a life-threatening situation, the moment might well arrive when you could do with a little advice on how to get out. And that's where this book comes in.

In these pages, you will find hints, tips, and how-to's on the art of surviving everything from a heat wave to a rock fall to a shoot-out to a wildfire to a mob riot to a tornado to a shark attack. In other words, pretty much the standard range of situations you are likely to encounter during a typical day in South Africa.

Before we move on, and just in case you already are in the path of a charging elephant, please would you be so kind as to take a deep breath and read the following item:

Disclaimer

Notwithstanding the fact that the information and advice contained in this book is believed, in all good faith, to be accurate, truthful, and recommended by a variety of experts who have lived to tell the tale, neither the author, cartoonist, publisher, proprietor, nor any other party directly or indirectly concerned with the making of this book, can accept any responsibility, legal or otherwise, should any of the survival advice contained herein be shown to not actually work. Thank you.

Now that we've got that out of the way, let's move on to the important stuff. This book would not have been possible without the kind and generous support of the fine people at Discovery Health. A warm thank you in particular to Adrian Gore, Barry Swartzberg, Neville Koopowitz, and Suzanne Stevens.

Thank you also to Rico Schacherl, Stephen Francis and Harry Dugmore of Rapid Phase, and to Zann Hoad of Sharp-Sharp Media, for their creative contributions, insights, energy and assistance in turning a casual idea into an actual survival handbook.

Much gratitude to Joey Monson for her fearless research, which included hanging out with lions, canoeing through rapids, clinging onto rock faces, and learning at first hand how not to be hijacked. Thank you to the survival experts who gave freely and willingly of their time to ensure the accuracy of the information in this book. (Please see under 'Acknowledgments' for a full list of names.)

And finally, a huge and heartfelt thank you to Madam, Eve, and Mother Anderson, who managed to find some time in their hectic print and television schedule to star in these pages. Okay, that's it. Read on, and whatever you do, happy surviving!

Gus Silber

Johannesburg

Eat Like a Bird.

Even under the best of circumstances, the age-old rule of "eat less food, more often" is a wise one to follow. But when the heat is getting out of hand, it's all the more important to avoid heavy meals that are high in fat and protein. One of the less-pleasant side-effects of a heat wave is the increased possibility of food poisoning.

Stay Out of the Sun.

Ignore this simple injunction at your peril, as Noel Coward more or less said in his famous song about Mad Dogs and Englishmen. When the mercury hits 40 degrees, a touch of sunburn can quickly turn to an attack of heat stroke. Stick to artificial climates, where the shade is generous and the air conditioning is always on high.

Watch Out for the Symptoms.

Your body will warn you when its built-in cooling mechanisms begin buckling under the strain of too much sun. If you feel the early aches and spasms of heat cramp, retreat immediately to a cooler place, rest, and replenish yourself with water. If your symptoms are rapid, shallow breathing, hot-to-the-touch skin and a weak pulse beat, call the medics – you've got heat stroke. You'll need to be immersed in a cool bath, wrapped in wet sheets, or otherwise cooled down as quickly as possible.

Drink Like a Fish.

Glug plentiful amounts of water, even if you don't feel particularly thirsty. Avoid coffee or alcohol, which will make you feel better for a while, but will intensify the dehydrating effect of excessive heat on your body.

CHEERS.

DRINK LIKE A FISH

HUMPH.

...BUT AVOID COFFEE OR ALCOHOL.

HOW TO SURVIVE
A BLIZZARD

Snow, the white, powdery substance that falls on the Drakensberg and makes it freezing cold in Gauteng, is a thing of wonder and a joy to behold in small doses. As any emigrant to Toronto will be able to confirm, the novelty wears off soon after the first snowball of winter gives way to the first snow shovel, the first power cut, and the first set of snow chains for your 4x4.

In our mercifully milder African climes, you may have to go out of your way to be caught in the grip of a bona fide blizzard. Unless, of course, you already stay on the border of the Free State and Lesotho, the Ceres district of the Cape, or some of the more elevated regions of KwaZulu-Natal.

Here's what to do when your pleasant outing to a winter wonderland is interrupted by a sudden onslaught of the cold, wet, white stuff.

Try Chilling Out for a While.

In most extreme situations, the key to survival lies in the swiftness of your reflexes and reactions. But when you're caught in a blizzard, you need to methodically, meticulously plan and think through every small move you make. Cold wears you down and tires you out fast. As the Eskimos say, and they should know: "You will get tired – the cold never will."

Try chilling out for a while.

Find Shelter Before You Find Your Way.

Trying to find your way in a snowstorm is like, well, trying to find your way in a snowstorm. Since you're up against a killer combination of cold, wetness and wind, shelter should be your first priority. If you've got a tent, you're in luck, but tie a part of it to yourself to prevent it from blowing away. If all you've got is your bare hands and the clothes on your back, dig a hole in the snow, away from the wind, preferably in the lee of a rock or the hollow around the trunk of a tree.

Wrap Up Nicely.

Presumably, if you are caught in a blizzard you will not be dressed for the beach. Then again, winter weather has a habit of taking South Africans by surprise. So maybe you will not be wearing the requisite multiple layers of fleecy clothing, topped by a wind- and waterproof outer garment. In which case, focus your attempts at insulation on your head. That's where most of your heat gets lost. And that's where you will have to do most of your thinking.

Eat a Lot of Stuff That's Bad for You.

If you're fortunate enough to have foodstuffs on your person, make sure they're of the variety not recommended by the Heart Foundation. Chocolate, biltong, boerewors, chips: anything high in oil and saturated fat. Think of your body as a car that normally travels at 60km/h. Now that it's cold, it's travelling at 200km/h. What it needs is fuel, and plenty of it. You can always go back on your diet later.

If You're Out of Water, Try Drinking the Snow.

The extreme cold may disguise the fact that you are dehydrating, but you need water in a snowstorm as much as you need it in the desert. If you're desperate, use your body heat to melt some snow.

Do Not Fall Asleep.

If you don't have adequate shelter, fight as hard as you can to stay awake. If you fall asleep, you will very quickly freeze and die.

Build a Snow Cave Next to Your Car.

If you're driving when the blizzard strikes, pull over and wait till it clears. But not necessarily in your car: you'll be better off building a "snow cave" next to your vehicle, and sheltering there.

Stay On the Wagon.

Avoid alcohol of any kind. It will lower your body temperature, which is the last thing you need in a blizzard. Try to erase the image of a St Bernard trudging through the snow with a keg of brandy around its neck.

Stay off the wagon.

HOW TO SURVIVE A TORNADO

In the searing heat of a summer day, a sudden, eerie stillness fills the air. Lightning flickers in the distance. A fleeting whip of wind sends a dust devil whirling down the street. Clouds gather, and the sky darkens to a strange greenish-grey.

Without warning, hailstones as big as marbles begin plummeting to earth. Windows shatter, trees shed their leaves. The storm stops. Silence. Followed by a low rumbling sound, like a freight train rolling down the tracks. Then, roaring across the landscape, comes a giant, funnel-shaped cloud, swallowing up everything in its path. Tornado.

Although South Africa is less prone to these whirlwinds of the Apocalypse than, say, Kansas, there were 185 "tornado events" recorded across the country during the previous century.

In Bethal in 1978, a petrol-tanker was lifted into the air and hurled a few metres; in Utrecht in 1993, a four-ton harvester became airborne; in Bronkhorstspruit in 1949, a flock of chickens were completely stripped of their feathers. How do you survive this kind of weather? The answers are blowing in the wind.

Don't Pin Your Hopes on the Weatherman.

Tornadoes are notoriously difficult to predict with any degree of accuracy. At best, according to the Weather Bureau, you can hope for a warning "20 minutes before touchdown". Generally, your first inkling will be an unusually intense hailstorm, followed by that train-like rumble and a roar like a Boeing about to take off.

Don't pin your hopes on the weatherman.

Watch the Direction of the Funnel.

If you've got a clear view of the tornado, and it's still some way in the distance, you may want to watch it for a few seconds, relative to a fixed object such as a tree or telegraph pole. If the funnel seems to be moving to the left or right, it's moving away from you. (For now.) If it seems to be staying in one place, and it's growing larger – watch out. You're right in its path.

Get Yourself Into a Rut.

If you're outside when you spot the funnel-shaped cloud, try to find yourself a hole in the ground. A ditch, a culvert, or a depression, preferably out of reach of easily uprootable trees. Lie flat, and cover your head. If it's raining, be aware that your misery may be compounded by a sudden flash flood.

Never Try to Outdrive a Tornado.

Since a tornado can travel at speeds of up to 300km/h, and can change direction with the will of the wind, abandon the thought that you can drive away from it in time. (This applies even if you are a minibus-taxi driver.) Stop, get out, and take cover immediately. Stay away from the road, because of the very real danger of low-flying vehicles.

Go down Below

A cellar, basement, or similar sub-surface structure will offer the safest form of shelter from the storm.

Remember to take a battery-operated torch with you, because the power lines in your neighbourhood will almost certainly be down.

Head for the Smallest Room in the House.

If you don't have a cellar, basement, or similar sub-surface structure, seek shelter in a wall-cupboard, stairwell, or, ahem, "bathroom". Wrap yourself in a coat or blanket as protection from flying debris. You can also try hiding in the bath with a mattress or sleeping bag over your head. In a school, shopping centre, or office building, head for small interior rooms on the lowest floor. Crouch as low as you can, ideally under a piece of stable furniture. And keep well away from the windows.

IT SAYS HERE WE SHOULD HEAD FOR THE SMALLEST ROOM IN THE HOUSE!

TORNADO SURVIVAL

EVERYBODY INTO EVE'S ROOM!!

Head for the smallest room in the house.

HOW TO SURVIVE
A SEISMIC EVENT

All right, then, an earthquake. Whatever the semantic niceties, there can be few sensations as terrifying as the feeling that the ground beneath your feet is about to tear into two.

While earthquakes of the Hollywood variety – tall buildings toppling, giant, steaming fissures opening up and swallowing people whole – are extremely rare in South Africa, man-made tremors are an everyday fact of life in the mining areas of Gauteng and the Free State.

Most of these measure around 2 on the Richter Scale, and are deadly only to those brave souls who earn their living below the surface. A "destructive earthquake" is anything above 6 on the scale. South Africa's worst example in recent memory: the 6.5-magnitude quake that shook the Tulbagh-Ceres area of the Cape in 1969, killing nine people and injuring many more.

Since sudden shifts in the earth's crust are impossible to predict with any degree of accuracy, the following tips may come in handy, particularly if you are planning to emigrate to San Francisco.

Don't Rush Outside to See What all the Noise is About.

If you're indoors when the earth starts moving, stay indoors until it stops. Take cover under any item of furniture that looks capable of absorbing the impact of falling debris. And be careful when re-emerging. You don't want to survive the trauma of an earthquake, only to knock yourself out on the underside of a solid oak table.

Take cover under any item of furniture that looks capable of absorbing the impact of falling debris.

Stand in a Doorway, but Watch Out for the Door.

Doorways are among the few structures likely to be left standing when the walls of your house come tumbling down. If your household furniture consists chiefly of coffee tables, scatter cushions and futons, the frame of a doorway will offer some protection. But mind the door. This is one time you don't want it slamming shut in your face.

Stay Away from Windows.

Even if you're just trying to get some amateur footage for the evening news, the spectacle of nature venting its fury will not be worth the prospect of being punctured by flying shrapnel. For the same reason, keep your distance from mirrors, glass partitions, display cabinets, and anything else that could shatter and fall.

On the Other Hand, Don't Rush Inside, Either.

Your instincts may tell you to dash into the nearest building when buildings start collapsing all around you. You're better off in the great wide open, as long as you stay away from power lines, skyscrapers, and – in the country – tall trees. If there's nowhere to take cover, sit or crouch with your hands shielding your head and face. Don't worry about the earth opening up and swallowing you whole. That only happens in the movies.

Stay in Your Car, but Try Not to Park On a Bridge.

If you're out driving when the sky starts falling, pull over and stay put, preferably keeping a low profile on the floor of your car. Don't drive around looking for parking, but don't stop on a bridge or freeway flyover, either.

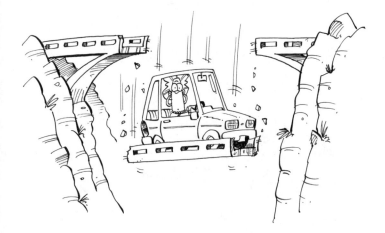

Stay in your car, but try not to park on a bridge.

HOW TO SURVIVE A FLOOD

Floods hold a special place in the mythology of disaster. From Noah to Atlantis to Mesopotamia to Mandingo, almost every culture has a tale to tell of a Great Deluge that destroyed the earth, whether through retribution, misfortune, or a simple, fleeting impulse to wipe the slate clean and create the world anew.

Head for higher ground.

In the real world, floods are rarely that devastating, but they are more frequent, as evidenced by the deluges that have battered almost every part of South Africa over the last century or so.

Perhaps the worst example was the flash-flood that hit the small Karoo town of Laingsburg in 1981, killing 104 people and leaving only 21 homes undamaged. If it can happen in the Karoo, it can happen anywhere, so here's what to do when that welcome downpour turns out to be not so welcome after all.

Get the Sandbags Ready.

If you have sufficient warning of a flood, sandbags will be your first line of defence against rising waters. You'll either be provided with the regulation trench-style variety by police or the army, or you'll have to fashion your own by filling plastic bags or pillowcases with earth or gravel. Stack the sandbags outside doors and windowsills. Use bits of old carpet or clothing if you run out.

Switch off the Power.

Water and electricity make very poor bedfellows. Rather than wait for a practical demonstration of this irrefutable scientific fact, get out the candles, torches, battery-operated radio and generator, and cut the mains before water starts rushing into your property.

Get Out While You Can.

Because of the unpredictable nature of floods, you may be ordered to leave your property while it's still dry and habitable. Don't argue. Sandbag, lock up, and go.

Head for Higher Ground.

This being the instinctive reflex of any animal or person caught in a deluge, you probably won't need reminding to head for the hills. If there aren't any around, or if the flood waters are too strong, dress warmly, grab a strong rope and a bright piece of cloth, and wait on your roof until the helicopters arrive.

Stay Put.

In the recent heavy floods in Mozambique, even people perched on tree tops in the midst of raging rivers managed to survive, thanks to the heroic efforts of airborne rescue teams. You're a lot better off sitting tight than trying to swim, drive, walk, or "raft" your way to safety.

Never Drive through Flood Water.

One of the most dangerous places you can be during a flood is behind the wheel of your car. You probably won't be able to see the road, and the road might not even be there. The pressure of flowing, rising water can engulf your car and sweep it away within seconds. If your car stalls during a flood, abandon it immediately and seek higher ground.

Watch Out for Snakes and Spiders.

As if one plague isn't enough, you might find your home invaded by reptiles, spiders, and other waterlogged creatures seeking sanctuary from the storm. Don't let them worry you too much. After all, they didn't worry Noah.

Fill Your Bath with Water.

Cold will do – you're not going to be bathing in it. For all the water, water everywhere, your municipal water supply is likely to be cut off or contaminated during a flood, and you'll need all the backup you can get. Fill every container, bucket and tub you can find as well.

Use your bath as an emergency water reservoir.

HOW TO SURVIVE A WILDFIRE

Dry weather, wind, fynbos, a tiny flicker of flame. Put them together, and you have a guaranteed recipe for a fire that will spread like, well, wildfire, as residents of the Cape Peninsula discovered during the devastating series of blazes that raged across the mountains for six days in January, 2000.

Dozens of homes were destroyed, over 20 per cent of the natural vegetation was turned to ash, and the insurance industry was left to pay out an estimated R4-billion in claims. The cause of it all? Most likely a cigarette tossed out of a car window.

Watch where you toss that match.

Of course, wildfires aren't restricted to the Western Cape, and are just as likely to occur when conditions are right in the forests of Mpumalanga, the veld of Gauteng, or anywhere else where a stray bolt of lightning or a careless spark can put the torch to our fragile natural environment. Here's what to do if you happen to be in the vicinity.

Build a No-Fire Zone Around Your Home.

If you stay near a forest, veld, or similar patch of combustible vegetation, you can reduce your exposure by building a "fire-safety zone" around your property. This means clearing all leaves, twigs, and other flammable material within a radius of at least 20 metres, pruning trees, mowing the lawn regularly, getting rid of old newspapers and rubbish, and making sure your garden hose is long enough to reach any part of your home and outbuildings in an emergency.

Get Ready to Get Out.

If wildfire threatens, don't stick around to fight it. Seal your property as best you can – shut doors and windows, move furniture to the middle of the room, lock up – and head for safety by foot or by car, taking careful note of the direction of the flames. Wear cotton or woollen clothing, a long-sleeved shirt and trousers, sensible shoes, and a damp handkerchief or cloth to protect your face. Be sure to tell a friend or relative outside the area that you've left your place and are safe.

Move Upwind.

By nature, the spread of a wildfire is as swift as it is unpredictable. Your best chance of escape is to move upwind, diagonally away from the path of the flames, and into an expanse of land that is devoid of vegetation, such as a rocky outcrop or cleared field. If things look desperate, head for the nearest natural body of water – a pond, a river, a stream – and crouch there until the flames subside.

Hit the Dirt.

If you're caught in the middle of a wildfire, lie flat on the ground, cover yourself as much as you can with wet clothing or soil, and breathe through a cloth or handkerchief to avoid inhaling smoke and scorching your lungs.

Do Not Leave Your Vehicle.

Given the choice between driving through a wildfire or running through it, choose driving. The risk of your petrol tank going up in a ball of fire has been greatly exaggerated by every Hollywood disaster movie you've seen.

Do not leave your vehicle.

2
ANIMALS RUNNING WILD

HOW TO SURVIVE
A CROCODILE ATTACK

Crocodiles, like sharks, are nature's way of telling you to avoid swimming in any body of water that does not come equipped with a Kreepy-Krauly.

If you don't mind taking the risk, or you inadvertently stray too close to the lair of a Nile Crocodile – and in South Africa, that includes rivers, lagoons, swamps, lakes and estuaries – it pays to know exactly what kind of creature you're dealing with.

A fully-grown Nile Crocodile can weigh up to 1,000kg, and reach a length of six-and-a-half metres. It will have 30 to 40 razor-sharp, interlocking teeth in each jaw, giving it the power to crush the bones of small animals, or seize an adult Cape Buffalo from the edge of a waterhole.

Bottom line: crocodiles deserve respect. But if it's a little too late in the day to give them that, here are some other techniques you may wish to apply.

Poke it in the Eye With a Sharp Stick.

Crocodiles attack swiftly and without warning. If you're the target, your only immediate advantage is your opposable thumb, and your ability to wield a weapon. A sharp stick is good; a hunting knife is better. If nothing else comes to hand, an index finger will do just as well. Jab it in one or both eyes. Hard. The crocodile should loosen its grip long enough for you to get away.

Pull the Crocodile by its Tail.

Before dragging its prey under water and tearing it to pieces through rapid rotation – the notorious "death roll" – a crocodile will often use its powerful tail to deliver the first blow. If you can pre-empt that tactic by grabbing hold of the tail and pulling as hard as you can, you'll throw the crocodile off balance and force it to let go of its prey. Note: this will work better when someone else is the prey.

Grab hold of the tail and pull as hard as you can.

Aim for the Part of the Body that isn't Protected by Armour.

Even the most armour-plated of reptiles must have a soft spot somewhere. You'll find it just behind the front legs, in the vicinity of the throat. Use any available weapon to pierce the soft, scaly skin, and you could do enough damage to save your own hide.

Ram Your Fist Down the Crocodile's Throat.

Your best chance of survival in a crocodile fight is to keep your head above the water. If you're losing the battle, and you're about to be plunged down below and rotated, try to ram your arm all the way down the crocodile's throat. There's a delicate membrane at the back of the neck, that keeps water from cascading into the lungs. Break it. The crocodile will instinctively rise to the surface, to keep from drowning. And so will you.

Do Not Disturb the Water.

Contrary to popular belief, crocodiles are not deterred from attacking by copious noise and large gatherings of people. Quite the opposite: they're attracted by commotion. Their acute sense of hearing leads them to scenes of splashing and bathing, where the element of surprise and the law of averages will heighten the chances of a successful attack.

Ram your fist down the crocodile's throat.

HOW TO SURVIVE
AN ELEPHANT CHARGE

Crashing through the undergrowth, tearing down the overgrowth, the African elephant is a humbling reminder of our middling-to-insignificant place in the food chain. Left to disturb the natural environment at its own leisurely pace, this largely placid herbivore presents no threat to the casual – and respectful – observer.

But a cow elephant in a breeding herd, or a bull elephant in the highly agitated state known as musth (a term best left unpronounced, since you will rarely need to use it in polite company) is another story altogether.

Rather than attempt to identify such animals by their appearance or behaviour, it is safest to assume that all wild elephants are territorial, unpredictable, and a whole lot faster and bigger than you. Here's what to do – and not to do – when the biggest of the Big Five starts heading meaningfully in your direction.

Take Charge of the Situation.

When you catch sight of a nearby elephant catching sight of you, the first thing you must do is freeze to the spot. This will require copious amounts of raw courage or cold fear, but it will give you time and space to gauge the elephant's intentions. All right, the elephant's charging.

Now what? Look closely: if the ears are spread out, the trunk is up, and the elephant is trumpeting, it is in all likelihood a mock charge. If the ears are back, the trunk is tucked away, and the elephant is ominously silent, it's the real thing. Time to get out of the way, quick.

Don't Even Think of Running.

Top speed of an elephant: 40 kilometres per hour. World record for 100m sprint: 9.88 seconds. But that's on a straight track, with no trees, thorn bushes, rocks or ant hills in the way. It stands to reason, therefore, that you should never attempt to outrun a charging elephant, whatever your own survival instincts may tell you. Indeed, old Africa hands advise that you should never attempt to outrun any wild animal other than a tortoise. Which is why they're old Africa hands.

Don't even think of running.

Get Out of the Way, Quick.

There are two basic ways to avoid the full impact of an elephant charge. The one is confrontation, the other is deviation. For confrontation, you will need an elephant gun and a steady eye and hand. For deviation, you will need to dive out of the way at the last second, and stay exactly where you land. Don't move a muscle. The elephant will assume you are dead, and will most likely move away.

Wrap Yourself Around a Tree.

In most cases, an enraged elephant will kill through a combination of tossing, goring and pulverizing. If all else fails, your best option is to get as close to the base of a tree as possible. The elephant will struggle to get hold of you, and may take out its frustrations on the tree instead.

Throw Something in the Air and Yell "YEE-HAAAAAA!"

You can also snap your bush-hat in your hands, to imitate a rifle shot, or unfurl a large umbrella to increase your apparent size. These tactics are the human equivalent of a mock charge, and should not be attempted if you do not possess a strong sense of the theatrical.

Always Stand Downwind of an Elephant.

Elephants can smell a lot better than they can see, so if you're upwind when you encounter one, move downwind as quickly and as quietly as you can.

HOW TO SURVIVE A CHARGING HIPPOPOTAMUS

Short, stout, pot-bellied, pig-eyed, covered with oily red secretions that are sometimes mistaken for blood, the hippopotamus is generally believed to be Africa's most dangerous animal.

Although there is a strong case to be made for the Cape Buffalo, the hippopotamus (somehow, "hippo" seems a little too familiar) deserves its reputation on the strength of its crushing bulk, its monstrous jaws, and razor-sharp canines that can reach up to 50cm in length.

Aside from everything else, hippopotami have the charming habit of marking their territory through copious defecation, which they spread with a propeller-like action of their tail. Zoologists refer to this practice as "dung showering". While the distinctive *hmmm-hmmm* of a hippopotamus in its amphibian lair is one of Africa's most evocative sounds, you are well advised to admire these beasts through the distance of binoculars.

Here's what to do in the event of a closer encounter.

Be Wary of Nice Pathways Leading to the River.

You might meet a hippopotamus coming up or down the path, since there is a good chance that the hippopotamus made the path in the first place. It is especially unwise to stand in the way of a hippopotamus on its way to the water, although you probably won't be standing there for long.

Be wary of nice pathways leading to the river.

Dive Behind a Bush.

Once again, the rule of "don't run from a wild animal" applies. A hippopotamus can reach a speed of 25 kilometres per hour, and can weigh as much as 3,200kg. Like elephants, they are unable to jump, but they're quite capable of charging up river banks to reach you. Dodge, dive, and stay down is the preferred strategy for survival.

Learn What Makes a Hippopotamus Angry.

If you are sitting on a river bank, and you see a hippopotamus rising to the surface, don't worry too much; it will not rush out and attack you. But if it's a bull and you're in its territory, or it's a cow with a calf, prepare to take evasive action immediately.

Never Sneak Up on a Hippopotamus.

Being amphibian, hippopotami are equally capable of attacking on water and on land. If you're out boating, perhaps in a mokoro or an inflatable raft, make a noise or tap the boat to alert any submerged hippopotami to your presence. They have a habit of upending vessels from below, or destroying watercraft with a single bite. If you see hippopotami in your vicinity, give them a very wide berth. They deserve to be treated with caution and respect at all times.

Always Stamp Out Your own Campfires.

Many tales have been told, usually around campfires, of the well-known hippopotamus habit of rushing up to campfires and stamping them out. While no wild animal enjoys a fire in its territory, these tales can be taken with at least a grain of salt. But keep an eye open, just in case. Hippopotami will travel several kilometres from their waterfront base in search of vegetation at night, and you might just be blocking the preferred route.

Be sure to alert submerged hippopotami to your presence.

HOW TO SURVIVE
A SHARK ATTACK

Just when you thought it was safe to characterise sharks as savage, bloodthirsty killing machines with an unquenchable penchant for human flesh, rest assured that these magnificent marvels of marine evolution present no threat whatsoever to any human who is wise enough to stay out of the ocean.

Misunderstood, maligned, harvested for soup, cosmetics and health food, sharks are available in some 370 varieties, from the compact cookie-cutter to the mega-mouthed megamouth. But in the context of "attack", a shark is generally understood to refer to the Great White, Tiger and Zambezi species.

Even these most aggressive of sea predators are undeserving of their reputation as indiscriminate man-eaters. Between 1965 and 2000, an average of three humans a year were attacked by sharks in South African waters. Less than ten per cent of the injuries were fatal. Statistics show that you're more at risk in the late afternoon, in murky water, in the Eastern and Western Cape, and if you're surfing or spear fishing at the time.

Bearing the odds in mind, here's what to do if you hear the sudden, unmistakeable sawing of a cello when you're next enjoying a relaxing paddle in the ocean.

Slink Off Like a Seal.

Most shark-attack victims don't see the shark until after they've been attacked. If you see a sizeable shark circling you, you've already won half the battle, because the shark will have surrendered its critical element of surprise. You will be assumed to be a seal or dolphin, and therefore capable of making a swift escape. Seize the advantage, keep the shark in your sights, and swim smoothly back to shore or the boat. If you panic or thrash around, the shark will assume you are an injured seal or dolphin, which puts you in a different category altogether. Food.

Swim smoothly back to shore or the boat.

Keep Out of the Feeding-Bowl.

As tantalising and evocative as the experience may seem, avoid the temptation to swim amidst a large school of fish. These schools will appear as dark, bubbling masses, cruising along the coast in search of food. Which makes them ideal feeding ground for bigger fish in the food chain. Don't be surprised if you get caught up in the feeding frenzy.

Try Not to Bleed.

Sharks can smell one part of blood in one million parts of water. Sharks (with the exception of plankton-feeders like megamouth) are carnivorous. That's pretty much all you need to know.

Punch it on the Nose, Poke it in the Eyes, Pull it by the Gills.

If you find yourself "bumped and bitten" by a shark, your best chance of survival lies in immediate, unexpected retaliation. Don't bite back: use your evolutionary advantage and fight dirty. A sharp jab on the nose or a poke in the eye should do the trick. Otherwise, grab onto the gills and pull hard. The idea is not to torture the shark, but to give it enough of a reason to let you go.

Get Your Wound Seen To.

Early first aid is crucial for shark-attack victims. Once you've reached shore, you need to stem the flow of blood by any means possible: wrap clothes or dry towels around the wound, and don't let sand get into it. Fortunately, lifeguards on most South African beaches will have special "Shark Attack Packs" within easy reach. All the more reason to confine your ocean-going activities to designated areas, within peak hours.

Use your evolutionary advantage, and fight dirty.

HOW TO SURVIVE A SNAKEBITE

Revered as symbols of healing and immortality, reviled as instigators of our original fall from grace, snakes have always enjoyed an uneasy relationship with our species.

Snakes have always enjoyed an uneasy relationship with our species

They may be capable of crushing us in their coils and swallowing us whole (African Rock Python), injecting us with a dose of neurotoxin that can paralyse and kill within 20 minutes (Black Mamba), and blinding us with a fine spray of venom from a distance of two metres (Mozambique Spitting Cobra), but for the most part snakes have enough of a sense of self-preservation to keep well out of our way.

Return the favour by treading with care in grassy, rocky areas, even if watching your step will not do you much good when there is a green mamba coiled around a branch above your head. Fortunately, of the 115 or so species of snakes in southern Africa, fewer than 30 are harmful to humans.

Learn to tell the difference between them, beginning with the basic rule that snakes with banded stripes are deadly, and snakes with longitudinal stripes are not. In the meantime, it's probably wisest to give every snake you meet a wide berth and the full benefit of the doubt.

Freeze in Your Tracks.

A snake will not attack a stationary target. If you stand completely still, or move ve-e-e-e-ery slowly, you will present no threat, and the snake will quickly lose interest in you. Even a Black Mamba, deadliest of Africa's serpentine predators, will slither over your foot and leave you alone if you get in its way and don't make a big issue about it.

Identify Your Attacker.

If you're unlucky enough to be bitten, endeavour to identify your attacker before you succumb to unconsciousness or delirium. Get a fix on colouring, size, markings and patterns if you don't know the name. Venomous snakes are categorised according to the broad effects of their venom: cytotoxic (tissue damage), neurotoxic (nerve damage), and haemotoxic (blood damage). Accurate identification will help you get appropriate treatment before it's too late.

Don't Get Too Excited.

It may not be easy to maintain your composure when you've just been pumped full of venom by a snake. But if you panic, you'll agitate your circulation, which will ease the absorption of venom into your bloodstream. For this reason, it's also very important that you do not raise your "bitten extremity" above the level of your heart. Corollary: try not to get bitten above the level of your heart.

Never Suck On a Snakebite.

Once again, it will only serve the purpose of spreading the venom around. (Also, it will leave a very unpleasant taste in your mouth.) Never try to cut or scrape the venom out with a blade, either.

Let it Bleed for a While.

You should let the bite bleed freely for about 30 seconds, before cleaning and disinfecting the area and applying a gauze dressing, followed by an overlapping crepe or stretch bandage. Do not apply too tightly, and definitely don't apply a tourniquet, especially of the makeshift variety (tie, belt, cord). It will restrict circulation, and you could lose the limb. Do not remove the dressing or bandage until your are at a facility where antivenom can be administered.

If you stand completely still, the snake will quickly lose interest in you.

HOW TO SURVIVE A LION ATTACK

Lionised for its strength, ferocity, hunting prowess and regal demeanour, the lion is in reality one of Africa's laziest animals, instinctively committed to conserving its energies, and capable of sleeping for up to 24 hours at a stretch. The lioness, of course, is a different story.

Nevertheless, lions of either variety are unpredictable and fiercely territorial, and should not be approached by anyone who is incapable of telling when they last had something to eat. (Lions eat once every seven to 10 days, so they're at their edgiest near the end of the cycle.)

Lions eat every seven to 10 days.

Lions in captivity can be even more dangerous than lions in the wild, due to their greater familiarity with humans, and the absence of a convenient outlet for their hunting instincts. Treat all lions with equal amounts of awe, respect and fear, and you may never have to apply the following bits of advice.

Talk Loudly to Yourself.

Because of their stealthy movements and superb camouflage, you may not know you're about to encounter a lion until it's too late. Better to let them know you're in the neighbourhood, by talking loudly and confidently to yourself as you move through the bush. Lions have an excellent sense of detection, and will generally retreat quietly if they know humans are approaching. But if a lion is sleeping – a fairly strong possibility at any time of day – you could take it by surprise. And vice versa.

Beware the Silent Charge.

If a lion charges towards you with a blood-curdling roar, try to stay exactly where you are. The charge will probably end a few metres away from you, and the lion will turn and leave you alone. If the lion is silent immediately before and during the charge, get ready to fight back. Lions do not roar when they're hungry.

Don't Run, Don't Climb a Tree.

Running from a charging lion – or even a non-charging lion – is an open invitation to a chase you have no chance of winning. Lions can sprint at 60km/h, and can bring down their prey with a single swat and a combination bite to the throat. Your best strategy is to back away, very slowly, while looking the animal in the eye. Don't climb a tree, either. Lions can climb faster and higher, although you do have an even chance that they won't be bothered to make the effort.

Carry a Sturdy Walking-Stick.

Even better, carry two. If the lion charges, shove one stick as far as it will go down its throat. Use the other to hit the lion hard on its back. By attacking the lion on two fronts (or at least, one front and one back) you should be able to incapacitate it sufficiently to make your escape. Warning: this technique only works on one lion at a time.

Offer the Lion an Arm.

With the lion thus preoccupied, you will be able to use your other arm to fight back, ideally with a knife in hand. Otherwise, punch, jab, throttle and pull for all you are worth.

Always let a lion know you are in the neighbourhood.

3

LIFE IN THE CITY

HOW TO SURVIVE A CROWD STAMPEDE

Fused from hundreds or thousands of separate individuals, a crowd is a multi-cellular organism that tends to act with single-minded purpose. Whether cheering on the competitors at a sporting derby, grooving in the "mosh-pit" at a rock concert, or chanting slogans at a political rally, crowds instinctively impose their own structure and discipline on proceedings.

You will not, for instance, see too many Chiefs supporters sitting in the Pirates section of the stands at FNB Stadium, and nor are you likely to see anyone sprinting the wrong way up the street during the annual "Running of the Bulls" in Pamplona.

But a single, unexpected incident – a scuffle, a gunshot, a trampled fence – can act as an instant catalyst for chaos, as the crowd scatters into its constituent parts and the law of momentum takes over. Short of avoiding large public gatherings altogether – by far the wisest move – here's what you can do if you ever get caught in a surge of uncontrollable humanity.

You are not likely to see anyone sprinting the wrong way up the street during the annual "Running of the Bulls" in Pamplona.

Veer to the Right or Left.

If you feel yourself being swept along by a mass of people, try to manoeuvre yourself to the edge of the crowd as quickly as you can.

Get to Know the Territory.

Before you settle down to enjoy the spectacle, take time to familiarise yourself with the lie of the land. Where are the exits? What do the colour codes mean? Where will you be able to congregate safely in the event of an emergency? Map out an exit route for yourself. If nothing else, it'll give you something interesting to do before the show begins.

Measure the Mood of the Crowd.

Sure, you're a part of it, but keep your eyes and ears peeled for any subtle shifts in mood. If you sense a growing agitation, or you just feel threatened or uncomfortable, try to head for more tranquil territory.

Watch Out for Bottlenecks.

It's human nature to rush to the front, and stake your claim to the best of all possible vantage points. But stay away from the clusters that form around fences, and resist the temptation to climb towers or walls. Remember: as high as you can climb, is as high as you can fall.

Get Into a Scrum.

If you're being pushed or shoved in a crowd, links arms with your companions and brace against each other, as if you're in a scrum. If you're by yourself, clasp your hands, extend your elbows, and bend forward slightly to give yourself room to breathe.

Assume the Foetal Position.

If you're knocked to the ground, and there are people surging all around you, bring your knees to your chest and make yourself as small as possible. Lie on your side, and use your hands and arms to protect your head and neck. Stay like this until you are absolutely sure the danger has passed.

HOW TO SURVIVE BEING STUCK IN A LIFT

Aside from its secondary function as a means of vertical transport, a lift is a small capsule of human neurosis at its most compelling. There is something about the process of being shafted from floor to floor, with only a set of flickering numerals as your guide, that can turn even the most stable of individuals into a suitable case for treatment.

You get the Obsessive-Compulsive, repeatedly jabbing the same button in the hope that this will improve the lift's speed of response. You get the Paranoid-Schizophrenic, convinced that at least one fellow-passenger is an escaped lunatic armed with a knife. You get the Pathological Exhibitionist, determined to share with everyone in earshot the details of a recent hernia operation.

Then you get the rest of us: the Lift-O-Phobics. Our only fear is that the power will fail, the cable will snap, the car will plummet, or – failing all that – we will step into the lift when the lift arrives, only to find that the lift isn't there.

Fear not. Help is on its way.

You get the Paranoid-Schizophrenic, convinced that at least one fellow-passenger is an escaped lunatic armed with a knife.

Press the Right Button.

It's the big one marked "Alarm". Speak clearly and calmly into the handset or intercom, and a technician will be along shortly. If there's no answer – maybe it's the weekend, or everyone's gone home – use your cellphone to call for help. You did remember to charge the battery, didn't you?

Don't Worry – the Cable Won't Snap.

The biggest myth about elevator emergencies is that the overhead cable will snap, sending the lift and its passengers plummeting into oblivion. In fact, modern lifts are supported by between four and eight steel hoisting ropes, each capable of holding the weight of a fully-loaded car on its own. On top of that – and at the bottom – a governing device and a pair of safety wedges will bring the car to a halt in the highly unlikely event of freefall.

Don't Try to Force Your Way Out Through the Overhead Hatch.

Sure, it works for Bruce Willis. In real life, alas, the emergency exit hatch is securely locked and can only be opened from the outside. This is to stop unqualified people from shimmying their way into the shaft, where they could slip on a patch of grease and land the owners of the building with a nasty lawsuit. For the same reason, don't try to prise the doors of the lift open with a Swiss Knife. You really need the Jaws of Life to be able to do that.

Don't Worry – the Lights Will Come Back On.

Even if there's a general power failure, modern lifts are equipped with some form of backup lighting supply, allowing you to identify the alarm button and read the bit of paper that tells you when the lift was last given the once-over by a Government Safety Inspector.

Sit Down, Relax, Make Yourself at Home.

Well, okay, the first part. Since the lift could lurch back into action at any moment, you might fall and injure yourself if you're standing. If the lift is crowded, make space for people who look like they really need to sit. You may have to wait a while, so occupy yourself with any activity that seems suited to a confined space. Reading, for example, or a communal sing-along.

Take the Stairs.

Not because it's safer. Just because you could use the exercise.

Occupy your time by singing a song.

HOW TO SURVIVE A MOB ON THE RAMPAGE

Under normal circumstances, society functions according to a set of systems and processes that are woven by mutual consent into the fabric of everyday life.

These include the principle that Red means Stop and Green means Go; that you drive on the left in South Africa; and that you walk on the pavement and cross the road only at safe and designated points if you are a pedestrian.

All well and good, until the moment you find yourself driving calmly down a city street, only to be confronted by a horde of angry, chanting pedestrians in the grip of a collective delusion that they – just for once – own the road. Here's what to do when a polite beep of the hooter fails to persuade them otherwise.

Go for the Gap.

There are three possible "mob on the rampage" scenarios. One: the mob is in front of you. Two: the mob is behind you. Three: the mob is all around you. Try to avoid scenario three altogether, by being aware of the direction of the mob, and making your getaway quickly and calmly through the nearest available gap.

Lock Your Doors, and Wind Down Your Windows Just a Little.

It's a good idea, of course, to drive with your doors locked at all times. If you've forgotten, this is where central locking or long arms will come in very handy. Try to wind down each window just a bit, as this will make them more flexible and harder to smash.

...TOLD YOU WE SHOULDN'T HAVE TAKEN THAT SHORT CUT.

Your safest bet may be to stop the car and sit tight.

Switch off Your Engine and Wait.

If you find yourself in the midst of a mob, you will have to carefully gauge their mood and intention. If it looks like they're just sweeping by on the way to someplace else, your safest best may be to stop the car, switch it off, and sit tight while the mass of humanity surges around you like the sea around a rock.

Rev Like Crazy and Mount the Kerb.

If you are confident of your advanced driving skills, or at least your advanced driving-like-crazy skills, the best way out of a mob crush may to be hit the revs as high as you can, mount the nearest kerb, and swerve off into the distance. You will need to build up as much speed and momentum as possible, or you'll just get stuck when the first wheel hits the pavement. When you swerve, be aware that the steering wheel will be ripped out of your hands, so make sure none of your fingers are wrapped around it. The natural human instinct for self-preservation should ensure that the mob parts as soon as you pop the clutch.

Become a Pedestrian Yourself.

If things start looking ugly, sitting in your car could turn you into a sitting duck. In which case, park wherever you can, even if it's right in the middle of the road. Lock your car, move calmly away, and seek sanctuary in a shop, doorway, or side street. Wait until it's completely safe to return to your car, and file your insurance claim as necessary.

HOW TO SURVIVE
A HOTEL FIRE

Havens of comfort and hospitality-for-hire, hotels offer the weary traveller or conference-goer a place to unwind, respite from the elements, and all the little luxuries your expense account can afford. But before you head for the mini-bar or pick up the phone to call room service, take a moment to peruse the piece of paper discreetly pinned behind your door.

It's the one that tells you what to do in the extremely unlikely event of a FIRE, and although you've seen it before, you've probably paid it as much attention as you normally pay the air hostess during the pre-flight safety briefing.

After all, modern hotels are equipped by law with overhead sprinklers, smoke alarms, fire-extinguishers and hoses, along with a full complement of trained personnel who know all the drills. But if you find yourself woken in the middle of the night by a shrill signal and the acrid odour of rising smoke, you'll feel a lot better if you know a couple of those drills yourself.

Plan Your Escape.

As soon as you've checked in, spend a few minutes checking out the quickest and easiest fire-escape route. Stroll down the corridor, and locate the nearest alternative exits and stairways. Count the number of doors and turns from your room. Note any obstacles that might get in your way. (Remember, you might have to do this on your hands and knees in a pall of smoke.) Locate the nearest fire alarm. Read the instructions. Then go back to your room and break the seal on your mini-bar.

Choose your room with care.

Leave Your Key Where You Can Find It.

Put it right there on the bedside table. You may need it to get back into your room if fire blocks your exit. Also, put your pocket flashlight within easy reach. (Never leave home without one.)

Roll Out of Bed.

If the smoke you smell happens to be in your own room, roll quickly out of bed and head for the door. Remember to grab your key and flashlight. Stay low, because of the risk of inhaling toxic fumes. Cover your nose and mouth with a wet cloth. Touch the door knob with the back of your hand. If it's hot, don't open the door. If it's not, open the door with extreme caution, and head for the nearest exit. Keep low if there's any smoke in the corridor.

Don't Take the Lift.

The Number One rule for surviving a fire in a high-rise building. The lift might well be working, but it could stop at a floor where the flames are raging out of control. Always take the stairwell, as long as it's clear of smoke. Hold on to the handrail. Not only for guidance, but to prevent you from being sent flying by panicking guests.

Put a Wet Mattress Against the Door.

If fire blocks your exit, it's probably safer to stay in your room. Call for help, and do whatever you can to keep the smoke at bay. Fill the bath with water. Soak towels and sheets, and put them around the door and air vents. Use your ice bucket to cool down the walls. Put your mattress against the door. Keep it wet. Open windows. Smash them if you have to. Signal to anyone out there. If you're higher than the first floor, don't even think of jumping.

Head for the Roof.

If you're on one of the higher floors, and you're trapped by a fire down below, head for the roof. It's one of the safest places to be in a hotel blaze, and you'll be easily visible to rescuers. Once again, be sure to take the stairs.

HOW TO SURVIVE
A TEAR GAS ATTACK

Battle-tested in the frontline of the Struggle against Apartheid, tear gas remains an essential item in the arsenal of any law and order unit called out to take care of an unruly mob. (Ruly mobs are generally quite capable of taking care of themselves.)

Even if you are innocently standing by while a street or campus protest is brought under control, a whiff of chloroacetophenone – the chemical most commonly used in tear gas – can reduce you to a crying, wheezing wreck with itchy, inflamed skin and an uncontrollably runny nose.

The effects can last from a few minutes to a couple of days, with more severe reactions in the case of infants, the elderly, asthmatics, and pregnant women. While proponents of its use regard it as a more humane and effective crowd-control measure than, say, sjamboks and German Shepherds, tear gas is officially listed as a toxic chemical weapon under the Geneva Protocol of 1969.

The following advice will come in handy when you next take part in an angry demonstration against the indiscriminate use of tear gas by South African security forces.

Watch Out for That Fruity Smell.

If you detect a distinctive bouquet of fruit or apple blossoms when you're in the vicinity of an angry crowd, it doesn't necessarily mean that Spring has sprung. What you're probably smelling is chloroacetophenone in its crystalline solid form. Enjoy it while you can: one of the common side-effects of tear gas is the temporary loss of your sense of smell.

Watch out for that fruity smell.

Cough, Spit, & Blow Your Nose.

The normal rules of public decorum do not apply when there's a riot going on. The coughing will be an involuntary reaction to the tear gas; the spitting and nose-blowing will help you get rid of the chemicals. Do NOT swallow, or your gastrointestinal tract will suffer the consequences for days.

Get Upwind.

Go where the air is fresh. Breathe deeply, slowly, and plentifully. But beware of too much sun: it will increase the irritant effect of the chemicals on your skin.

Flush Out Your Eyes With Water.

Tear gas can temporarily blind you, or leave you blinking uncontrollably. Resist every temptation to rub your eyes. Instead, flush them copiously under the nearest tap, shower, or hose pipe. If your eyes are sealed shut – it happens – get someone to apply cotton wool balls soaked with water. If you wear contact lenses, remove them with clean hands as soon as you can.

Don't Pick Up a Spent Tear Gas Canister.

It might look like an attractive souvenir, but you'll badly burn your hands if you're not wearing industrial-strength gloves.

Wear the Right Clothes.

If you're expecting a riot to break out, and you don't mind being part of the action, dress sensibly. Which means: no shorts, tee-shirts, or bikini-tops. The more layers of clothing you wear, wrapped tightly at the wrists, ankles and neck, the better you'll be able to protect your hide when the tear gas canisters start clunking. Try to avoid cotton or wool, which will absorb the tear gas and release it slowly for days afterwards.

The more layers of clothing you wear, the better.

4

THE GREAT OUTDOORS

HOW TO SURVIVE BEING LOST IN THE MOUNTAINS

In the wide-open spaces of our magnificent mountain ranges, far from the pollution, skyscrapers and traffic of the city, you can happily wander for hours and hours before coming to the conclusion that you are hopelessly lost.

Here, there are no street signs, no friendly policemen, no towering man-made landmarks to guide you. Here, you probably won't even be able to get a signal on your cellphone. (Indeed, the search for a signal may be the reason you got lost in the first place.)

Whether you're at large in the remote crags of the Drakensberg, or on the deceptively accessible slopes of Table Mountain, there is one factor that can turn your quandary from a mild inconvenience into a major disaster. And that is the fickle temper of Mother Nature.

One moment, the sun is shining in a cloudless sky; the next, you can't see your hand in front of your face. One moment, you're about to cross a gentle mountain stream;

the next, you're in the path of a raging torrent. Here's how to cope if you should lose your way when you next go to the mountains to find yourself.

If you're going to be lost, be lost together.

Tell Yourself You're Not Really Lost After All.

Being lost is a physical state that can quickly make you lose your mind. As your pulse races and your breathing quickens, you can descend into blind panic, confusion, and despondency. The trick is to stop, take stock of your surroundings, and remind yourself that you're not really lost, as long as you know what country, mountain range, or wilderness area you're in. It may not help much. But it's a start.

Pour Yourself a Nice Cup of Tea.

The traditional English antidote to a moment of crisis will serve you well when you've momentarily misplaced your way. Ideally, you will be in a party with at least two other people. Ideally, someone will have remembered to bring the kettle. Drink up, gather your strength and wits, and get ready to move on if the weather allows it.

Try to Retrace Your Steps.

It's all very well to take the road less travelled by, until you discover why it's the road less travelled by. If you stick to well-worn routes, with ordnance map and compass close to hand, you should be able to backtrack to the point where you went wrong. Note: remember to pack ordnance map and compass.

Don't Break Up the Party.

If you're going to be lost, it's better to be lost together than on your own. The party should only ever be split up if one of its members is injured, and someone else is confident of finding help.

Learn to Read the Signs.

Ignore the odd graffito which advises, "If you can read this, you're lost". Rather, look for moss, which tends to grow on the southern side of trees; weavers' nests, which are always built on the west side; and the sun, which helpfully never fails to rise in the east and set in the west.

Be Prepared to Get Lost.

Always pack extra food and water, appropriate clothing, some form of shelter, and enough bright material to pinpoint your position to passing helicopters. (You may not have the strength to spell out SOS in rocks.) Always fill in the mountain register before setting off, as well as when you return. And take a fully charged cellphone. Just in case.

Always pack extra food and water, appropriate clothing, and some form of shelter.

HOW TO SURVIVE
A DAY AT THE BEACH

For millions of landlubbers (and quite a few ocean-lubbers as well) there is no surer formula for rest and recreation than a day of sun, surf, sand and sea. From Umhlanga to Clifton to Plettenberg Bay, the marine environment holds a magnetic allure, partly connected to the swell of the tide, and partly to our instinctive desire to return to the scene of our evolution as a species.

The rules for enjoying a day at the beach are simple. Bathe in designated areas only, apply liberal amounts of sun block, don't swim on a full or empty stomach, never drink and dive, and always tread with care in the vicinity of giant concrete outflow pipes.

Having said that, it pays to be aware of one or two other seaside situations that can make you wish you'd stayed at home watching TV. Here's how to make sure they don't ruin your day.

Beware of Brainless, Spineless, Ocean-Going Creatures.

Mesmerising marvel of nature, the gelatinous, free-floating jellyfish is composed of 99 per cent water and one per cent organic matter. It has no heart, no brain, no backbone, and is devoid of any sense other than touch. But if you're touched by a jellyfish, or at least one of the 70 species that sting, prepare to be in agony for a while.

Immediately rinse the affected area with salt water – not fresh water, which will activate any stinging cells left on your skin – and detoxify the venom by sprinkling baking soda or meat tenderiser over it. Plain old beach sand is an acceptable but less effective substitute, while an ice pack (ice in a plastic bag) will help ease the pain. If the swelling doesn't go down, or you have difficulty breathing, get medical help quickly.

Never Swim Against a Rip Tide.

Even strong and experienced swimmers can be pulled out to sea by a rip tide, which is a current or undertow that often forms after a storm. They're also common around piers, which is a good reason to avoid swimming in their vicinity. If you get caught in the tide, resist your natural impulse to swim against it. Stay calm, go with the flow, and try to swim parallel to the shore. Otherwise, float with the current, until you're safely out of the rip. Then swim well away from it, and into calmer waters.

Stay Out of the Sun.

Even if you're oozing sun block, it isn't wise to worship the sun for more than half-an-hour at a time. This applies even if the sun is hiding behind cloud. Too much sun can quickly lead to dehydration and heat exhaustion. The symptoms: nausea, dizziness, red, itchy skin, and high body temperature. The treatment: get into the shade, drink plenty of water (no soft drinks or alcohol), and get someone to put a cool compress on your forehead. Then go inside and watch TV.

Watch Out For Flying Fish-Hooks.

There is something very soothing about standing on the shore and watching fishermen fish. But don't stand too close, or you could unwittingly be the catch of the day. To remove an imbedded fish-hook, wrap twine or line around the curve of the hook, at the point where it enters the skin. Push firmly on the shaft of the hook, and give the twine a quick, sharp tug. The hook should disengage. Clean and dress the wound, and seek medical attention if necessary.

Watch Out For Flying Fish-Hooks.

HOW TO SURVIVE BEING TRAPPED IN WHITE WATER

Combining the thrill of surging, churning torrents with the challenge of jutting rocks, overhanging branches and unpredictable currents, whitewater rafting is one of the finest ways of recovering from the stresses and strains of everyday urban life. Coping with the stresses and strains of whitewater rafting is another issue altogether, whether your vessel of choice is a one-person kayak or the inflatable equivalent of a fully loaded minibus taxi.

Southern Africa offers some spectacular locations for confronting white water, from the Great Zambezi to the gorges and canyons of the Orange and Fish rivers. Unless you accidentally fall into one of these treacherous stretches of water, you will presumably be there because your idea of a good time is trying to stay upright in a treacherous stretch of water.

You will also presumably be wearing a brightly coloured helmet, be part of an organised and well-equipped party, and have a thorough understanding of the difficulty levels of white water, which range from Easy (fast-moving water with small waves) to Expert (long, obstructed, or very violent rapids) to Extreme and Exploratory (don't ask).

Here's what to do when the waters turn against you.

Lose Your Boat Before Your Boat Loses You.

If there are dangerous rapids or rocks up ahead, your
instincts and experience should tell you whether you are
capable of surviving them. If in any doubt, release your
boat and attempt to swim to shore.

Lie face Up, With Your Feet Downstream.

If you're swimming in shallow or obstructed rapids,
orientate your body face up, with your feet pointing
downstream. This will allow you to fend off any
obstacles. Try to raise your rear as well, which will make
it easier to float over such obstacles.

Do Not Attempt to Stand in Fast-Moving Water.

Your feet may be wedged on the bottom, and you will be
pulled under and held there. Only attempt to stand or
walk in slow or very shallow water.

Watch Out for Strainers.

So-called because they can strain you in more ways than
one, "strainers" are branches, trees, or any other debris
that you may see draped into the water.

Do Not Hug the Rock.

It's human nature, when you're in peril, to grab hold of
the nearest solid object and hang on for dear life.

But getting "wrapped" against a rock by the force of the water will only make your position more perilous. As whitewater rafters are fond of saying, you will not get anywhere in life by sitting on a rock in the middle of a fast-moving river.

Don't Breathe Until You Can See the Clear Blue Sky.

It's easy to become disoriented when you are being held under a relentless torrent of white water. As you force your way to the surface, you may be tempted to start breathing when you see the bubbles all around you. This will be a mistake – you will be breathing water. Hold your breath until you can see the sky.

Be Very Wary of Weirs.

Weirs, being man-made, can be even crueller than natural patches of water. The water below a weir will be moving in a perfect circular motion, so if you fall into it, it'll be like being trapped in the spin cycle of a washing-machine. Your best option is to make yourself heavier, which means going against the current of safety advice and losing your life jacket. You should then be able to swim down and away from the weir, or sideways towards the bank.

HOW TO SURVIVE A LIGHTNING STRIKE

Whether seen from the comfort of a stoep in the Great Karoo, the patio of a penthouse in Sandton, or the back of a Landrover on the plains of the Sabi Sands, there are few spectacles as calculated to take your breath away as a lightning storm breaking over the wide-open African sky.

But if you're caught in the wrong place at the wrong time, a lightning strike could be the last spectacle you'll ever see. Lightning kills up to 200 people a year in South Africa.

Even if you do survive, the short- and long-term effects of a strike can range from blindness to deafness to amnesia. So don't tempt lightning. It may be true that it never strikes twice in the same place. But if it strikes you once, that's generally enough.

Get Out of the Open.

Lightning strikes occur most often on open patches of land, such as a golf course, football field or public park. If you're out in the open, STOP whatever you're doing and seek appropriate shelter. This applies even if you're playing golf. Sad as it may seem, your chances of being struck by lightning are significantly higher than your chances of scoring a hole in one.

Beware of Bolts from the Blue.

Don't wait until you see lightning, which can strike from a clear blue sky. Heed the warning of distant thunder. Get moving, and get under cover.

Shelter in a Building or Inside a Car.

When lightning strikes, you're safest in a building or inside a car, with the doors and windows closed. True, cars are made of metal, but they're ideally designed to deflect current and insulate you from harm. For this reason alone, you may wish to avoid driving an open-top convertible during a thunderstorm.

Avoid driving an open-top convertible during a storm.

Watch Out for That Tingly Feeling.

If you're outside during a storm, and you start getting a tingly sensation on the back of your neck, it doesn't mean you're psychic. It means lightning is about to strike in your immediate vicinity. Do NOT attempt to outrun it. (A lightning bolt can deliver one million volts of current in approximately one hundred-thousandth of a second.)

Instead, crouch into a ball, with your head down and your feet together. Wait for the lightning to pass. And then get under cover if you can.

Walk, Don't Run.

While it's wise to clear the scene as quickly as you can when there's lightning in the air, it's unwise to bolt like lightning. Running can generate static electricity, which can attract bolts from the blue. So walk briskly and calmly, ideally without any metal objects on your person. (Photographic tripods, metal-tipped umbrellas, spiked golfing shoes. Money's probably okay.)

Get Off the Water.

Lightning and water go together like, well, lightning and water. Head for shore immediately if you're swimming, boating or fishing. And if you're fishing, lose the rod.

Don't Huddle.

You may think, if you're out in the open with a big storm brewing, and there's no shelter in sight, that it's a good idea to huddle together with other people for safety.

Wrong. If lightning strikes one, it'll strike all. You need to keep a good five metres between yourself and the nearest person.

Never Shelter Under a Tree.

If only every nugget of parental advice were as easy to remember as this oft-repeated injunction. Trees can act as lightning rods during a storm. If you're sheltering under one, and it takes a hit, you're toast.

Trees can act as lightning rods during a storm.

HOW TO SURVIVE
A ROCK FALL

Stripped of the romantic delusion that we occupy a
special place in the cosmos, our planet is little more than
a big rock falling through space. (And not even a very big
rock, at that.)

With this is mind, it pays to remember that rocks of all
shapes and sizes are just as subject to the law of gravity,
and all its relevant sub-sections. Even a small rock, no
bigger than the size of your fist, can kill you if it falls
from a great enough height, at a great enough speed.

So when you're in the Berg, or anywhere else where
echoing crags resound, look out, look up, and remember
to duck. Rock falls are nowhere near as common in
South Africa as they are in Alpine territories, but they
still present enough of a threat to seal off a landmark like
Chapman's Peak Drive.

Here's how to keep your head when rocks are falling all
around you.

Beware of Baboons Bearing Rocks.

Driven by some primal, pre-evolutionary impulse, baboons and other lower primates find it hard to resist hurling rocks at humans passing down below. If you notice such creatures in an area where the rocks and the animals are known to be unstable, get ready to take evasive action. And that doesn't mean throwing rocks first.

Beware of Baboons Bearing Rocks.

Wear Something Hard On Your Head.

As the uppermost part of your body, your cranium presents the most obvious and immediate target for a cluster of rocks in freefall. Follow the example of test cricketers and human cannonballs, and put a lid on it. Modern helmets are made from lightweight polycarbonate, with foam padding, air vents, and a wide range of styles and colours to make you look and feel cool. So much so, that you may be tempted not to wear your helmet in case a rock falls on it.

Shout "Rock!" at the Top of Your Lungs.

If you spot a rock falling during a hike or climb with other people, the accepted thing to do is shout "ROCK BELOW!" in a very loud voice. This applies even if the rock is above; what is really means is, "watch out for rocks down below." You can also just yell "ROCK!" but only if you're certain that this isn't the name of a member of your party. If you hear someone else shouting a rock fall warning, the accepted thing to do is not look up to see which rock they're talking about.

Hide Yourself in a Depression.

Happy campers know that you're not supposed to camp out in a depression in the middle of a valley, because a sudden fall of rock from a spectacular surrounding mountain can really ruin your sleep. However, if rocks are already falling, a depression – such as a crevice or a hole in the ground – can be a good place to hide. Use as many limbs as you can to shield yourself, and wait until it's all over before you emerge.

Hug the Nearest Non-Moving Rock.

If you're climbing a big rock, of the variety that tends to stay in a fixed position for billions of years, get as close to its face as possible when smaller rocks start raining all around you. Rock climbers call this "hugging the rock", and it's based on the principle that a falling rock bounces OUTWARD from the face. You'll probably be using your hands for holding on, but if not, use them to protect your own face and neck.

Hug the nearest non-moving rock.

HOW TO SURVIVE BEING TRAPPED IN QUICKSAND

So there you are, enjoying a casual stroll along a beach front or forest trail, when you suddenly get the strangest feeling that the trees in the distance are growing taller before your eyes. Your gait, once jaunty and confident, becomes laboured and sluggish. You hear an odd plopping sound. You look down. Your knees have disappeared.

You're in quicksand. The substance of childhood nightmares, the morass that conveniently opens up to swallow bad guys in cowboy movies, leaving nothing but a black Stetson and a few feeble bubbles.

In truth, quicksand is a relatively benign amalgam of elements that has fascinated physicists for centuries. Even Albert Einstein wrote a paper on quicksand, presumably using a firm piece of cardboard as support. You'll find patches of quicksand wherever coastal or inland water meets terra-sort-of-firma, particularly in the Cape, the hills of KwaZulu-Natal, and in and around the quaint Lesotho village of Teyateyaneng, which means "Place of Quicksand".

The good news is that quicksand won't clamp your limbs and suck you into a bottomless pit. The bad news is that it can really ruin your hiking clothes. Here's how to get out of the stuff quick-quick.

The quaint Lesotho village of Teyateyaneng, which means "Place of Quicksand".

Tread Lightly, and Carry a Big Knobkierie.

Follow in the footsteps of the kind of hikers who never venture outdoors without a hand-carved walking-stick. Aside from being used to fend off snakes and wave "tally-ho" at fellow walkers, a stick will come in handy for prodding suspect soil, clay, marsh or silt. And if you fall in, you can always use it to lever yourself out.

Wear Sensible Shoes.

Avoid big, heavy boots, which will hinder your efforts to extricate yourself. Tennis shoes are much better, and are easier to slip out of, while going barefoot gives you the best anti-suction protection of all. But mind the thorns.

Don't Make a Splash.

Falling into quicksand is a lot like falling into water, albeit in slow motion. The same abiding principle of "don't panic" applies, especially since most quicksand will only reach as far as your knees or waist. (This will not be of much comfort if you are short.) Do not make any rapid, flailing movements, which will agitate the quicksand and aggravate your situation. Thinking quickly, and acting slowly, is the best way to get yourself out.

Lie Back and Take it One Foot at a Time.

Science lesson: if a solid object is placed in liquid, it will sink if its density is greater than that of the liquid. The solid object in this case is your body, which happily has a lower density than liquid. Stay calm, lie on your back, and you should easily be able to manoeuvre your way to firmer ground. Warning: if you are wearing a heavy backpack, your average density increases dramatically. Take it off, even if you have to let it sink.

Don't Forget to Breathe.

Filling your lungs with deep gulps of oxygen will increase your natural buoyancy, and make it easy for you to rise above the state you're in.

Rope Someone in to Help You out.

If you're heading for shaky ground, it's always a good idea to take a companion armed with a length of strong rope. (About 5m or more.) Failing which, a sturdy branch will do nicely. Just make sure you don't both fall in at the same time.

Rope someone in to help you out.

HOW TO SURVIVE A CHARGING BULL

Every summer, during the Festival of San Fermin in the northern Spanish town of Pamplona, hundreds of people from around the world demonstrate their courage and bravado by scrambling to get out of the way of a herd of young bulls. This is not to be confused with what happens next, which is a series of sporting contests between individual bulls and professional matadors. Well, sort of sporting.

Since bullfighting is banned in South Africa, few among us would have the presence of mind (not to mention the cape and the sword) to react in the recommended fashion when 650kg of prime beef comes hurtling towards us.

Unlike the female of their species, bulls do not generally suffer humans gladly. Especially humans who shouldn't be wandering in the field in the first place, or who, through generations of urban evolution, have lost the instinctive ability to tell the difference between a bull and a cow. Hint: a cow will allow you to roam freely in its pasture. A bull will charge.

Unlike the female of their species, bulls do not suffer humans gladly.

Learn to Talk Bull.

Or at least, to read it. A bull will communicate its aggressive intent through a series of unmistakable body-postures and gestures. These will usually begin with a "broadside threat display", in which the bull arches its back, lowers its head, and shakes it from side to side, with eyeballs protruding. Then comes the direct head-on threat, with shoulders hunched and neck curved to the side. Finally, the bull will paw the ground, and might also rub its horns in the dirt. By which time, you should have got the message.

Make Yourself Look Bigger.

By carrying a walking-stick, umbrella, pole, or cricket bat, you will appear larger to the bull, which should help to deflect the threat. If the bull is not fooled, the item can then be used as a weapon. Aim for right between the eyes. But only if you absolutely have to.

Never Turn Your Back On a Bull.

Sound advice, studiously ignored by the bull-running hordes of Pamplona. Then again, if you run in Pamplona, there will usually be at least one other runner between you and the bull.

Give the Bull Some Space.

Bulls have a "flight zone" of approximately six metres. If you're cornered by a bull, retreat slowly to this distance. And then retreat some more. But remember not to turn and run.

Wave a Red Flag.

Actually, it doesn't have to be red. Nor does it have to be a flag. Nor do you actually have to wave it. But if you have an item of clothing or material in hand, throw it in the bull's path. It will provide a moment or two of distraction.

Wave a red flag.

Dodge.

Like many large animals, bulls are good at charging, bad at steering. When a charge seems inevitable, and the nearest tree or fence is a long way off, swerve at the very last second. Keep doing this until you reach safety, and don't take your eyes off the bull for a second.

And While You're At It, Watch Out for Cows.

Although cows are docile by nature, they can exhibit bull-like behaviour when newborn calves are around. Don't take a chance; say "ag shame" from a distance.

5

TRANSPORT PROBLEMS

HOW TO SURVIVE
A HIJACKING IN THE AIR

So commonplace have vehicular hijackings become in South Africa, that we tend to overlook the fact that it is also possible to get hijacked in the air. The main difference is that airborne hijackers do not generally want to steal the plane; they merely wish to divert it to a different destination.

Airborne hijackers do not generally want to steal the plane.

This has been the case ever since the first hijacking in 1931, when a group of rebel soldiers in Peru tried to force two American pilots to fly over Lima and drop propaganda leaflets. The pilots refused. In history's only recorded case of self-hijacking, the pilot of an Air China flight diverted from Beijing to Taiwan in 1998, after threatening to kill all passengers and crew. The plane landed safely.

Hijackings are a lot less common today than they were in the Seventies and Eighties, thanks to increased security and the easy availability of scheduled flights to Cuba, Beirut, and other exotic destinations. But hey, you never know.

Try and Avoid the Aisle Seat.

If you usually choose an aisle seat, in the faint hope that this will grant you extra legroom and quicker access to the "cloakroom", be aware that this will make you a more obvious target for aggravation in the event of a hijacking. The aisle is also where most of the action will take place when the plane is stormed after landing. You'll also be safer at the rear of the plane, as far away from the cockpit as possible.

Plan Your Flight With Care.

Choose an airline with a good record for safety and punctuality. Try to book a non-stop flight, as this will lessen the chance of dodgy passengers boarding at airports with dodgy security. Be extra wary on domestic hops, favoured by most hijackers on the grounds that you don't need travel documents to fly internally.

Keep Your Seat Belt Fastened for the Duration of the Hijacking.

In other words, stay put and stay calm. Your hijackers are likely to be just as tense and nervous as you are, so don't give them an excuse to get all jumpy.

Obey All Reasonable Instructions.

You will probably be ordered to hand over your passport and belongings. You may be separated by sex, citizenship, or race. You may be asked to keep your head down or change your body position. Respond swiftly, even it seems unreasonable at the time. Remember, you are not the only passenger on board.

Don't Ask a Hijacker for an Extra Pillow.

Try to address any urgent requests for assistance to the nearest available crew member. Don't speak to a hijacker unless spoken to, and if so, respond in a neutral, carefully regulated tone, without getting into a conversation.

Get Ready to Duck.

If you hear shots from inside or outside the aircraft, get your head down or drop to the floor.

Everyone's a Hijacker Unless Proven Otherwise.

If you're lucky enough to be rescued by a crack squad on the ground, obey the instructions of the Good Guys with equal speed and diligence. Expect to be treated brusquely, if not roughly – "Get your hands behind your head NOW!" – until it is determined beyond doubt that you are merely an innocent passenger.

Give the Hijackers Nicknames.

Preferably not to their faces. Do it silently, based on your discreet observations of their physical characteristics, accents, mannerisms, and so on. (This may be difficult if they're all wearing balaclavas.) The information could come in handy at a later stage.

Give the hijackers nicknames.

HOW TO SURVIVE "ECONOMY-CLASS SYNDROME"

Forget the nightmare of turbulence at 30,000 feet. Never mind the prospect of an enraged passenger bursting into the cockpit. Don't even think about the food. The real danger to life and limb in long-distance flying is a killer so silent, so stealthy, that you may not even know you've come under attack until you step off the plane.

Your doctor will call it Deep Vein Thrombosis (DVT), but it's better known by its tabloid tag: Economy-class Syndrome. Here's what happens. You sit in one position for hours on end, hemmed in by the knees at your back and the back at your front, until a clot starts forming slowly in a deep vein in your body.

The clot breaks into small pieces, or emboli, which can travel through the heart and block the flow of blood to your lungs. Result: a pulmonary embolism, which can strike without warning and leave you dead within days. Economy-class Syndrome can affect an athlete in the peak of condition, just as easily as an overweight smoker with a history of heart trouble.

And here's the really bad news: it can even affect you if you travel First Class. Or, for that matter, if you're the pilot. Here's how to survive that looooong flight across the Atlantic.

Eat a Little, Drink a Lot (Of Water)

Dry air and high altitude can compound the effect of a sedentary position on your blood vessels. It's important to stay hydrated, but avoid coffee and alcohol.

DRINK A <u>LOT</u>...   ...BUT AVOID COFFEE AND <u>ALCOHOL</u>.

Exercise Any Muscle You Can Move.

Tough as it may be to clamber over your fellow passengers and squeeze past the food cart in the aisle, try to leave your seat and walk around for at least five minutes every hour. Otherwise, stretch your arms, extend your feet, and flex your ankles, toes and heels on a regular, rhythmic basis. Clots often form in the calf or thigh region, so don't forget to massage or activate the muscles there as well.

Don't Sleep for More than a Couple of Hours at a Time.

This shouldn't be too much of a problem, since it's usually impossible to sleep for more than a couple of minutes in Economy, anyway. Sleeping too long in a cramped position can increase your risk of developing a thrombosis.

Take Half an Aspirin and Call Me in the Morning.

Among its many other qualities, Aspirin in moderation is effective at thinning the blood. But speak to your doctor before you fly, especially if you fall into a high-risk category for thrombosis. That includes diabetics, pregnant women, and anyone who still has signs of bruising from a recent injury or surgery.

Get Yourself a Pair of Sensible Socks.

They're called Graduated Compression Hosiery, and they're made from special elastic threads that exert varying degrees of pressure to assorted parts of your leg. Hey, nobody needs to know.

Watch Out for the Symptoms.

Chest pain. Leg pain. Swelling of the leg or lower limb. Shortness of breath. Fainting spells. Vividly visible surface veins. Get yourself to a doctor quick, and next time, take the boat.

Watch out for swelling of the leg or lower limb.

HOW TO SURVIVE BEING SUBMERGED IN YOUR CAR

With the possible exception of the original VW Beetle, which was rumoured to be able to float for up to four hours because of its bubble-shaped, engine-at-the-back design, few modern cars are inherently equipped for amphibian action. You hit the water and you sink. Slowly.

It's probably the most nightmarish of all automotive emergency scenarios, and yet, it is the very delay in the process that gives you your best chance of surviving. Most modern cars will take a minute or two to sink, and up to half-an-hour to fill with water. This will give you time enough to plan your escape if you are uninjured and are able to think and act swiftly.

As much as it may fill you with a rising sense of dread, take a little time to think about it now.

Always Wear Your Seat Belt.

To the small but vocal anti-seat belt brigade, the prospect of being trapped in a cage of metal and glass under water is one of the most compelling reasons to ride strapless. But the argument falls flat when you weigh up the alternative: without a seatbelt, you're likely to be thrown around and knocked unconscious when your car hits the water at speed. So belt up, bearing one little caveat in mind.

Most modern cars will take a minute or two to sink.

Always Remember to Unbuckle Your Seat Belt.

In the panic and confusion that follow a collision with a body of water, it's easy to forget that you have to pop your seat belt before you can swim to safety. The recommended mnemonic is POGO: Pop the seat belt, Open the window, and Get Out.

Forget the Door, Try the Window.

If your car is sinking slowly enough, you should be able to wind down a window and escape. If the windows are electric, they probably won't work just when you need them most. But whatever happens, don't waste your strength trying to open a door. The pressure of thousands of kilograms of water from outside will make the task impossible.

Wait for the Pressure to Equalise.

It may sound crazy to sit and wait as the car fills with water. But it is only when the pressure is equal inside and outside, and the water level stops rising, that you will have a chance of opening the door. Until then, move to the rear of the vehicle, near the roof, where you should be able to find a small pocket of air to keep you going.

Carry a Centre Punch in Your Car.

A centre punch is a small, sharp, spring-loaded device that will shatter a window with a push, even under water. It will come in particularly handy if your electric windows have been short-circuited. Use it on a side window; it won't work on the tempered safety glass of your windshield or back window. A hammer will also do the trick, although it will require greater muscle. Carry both items in your cubbyhole, just in case. Do not leave them in your boot.

Turn On the Lights.

It's going to be dark and murky under water, so try to switch on the headlights and interior lights. There's a good chance they'll still be working. They'll help you find your bearings before you take a deep gulp of air and swim to the surface. Otherwise, they'll make it easier for rescuers to pinpoint your location.

HOW TO SURVIVE
AN AIRCRAFT CRASH

Safer than a quick trip to the corner café, safer than a minibus ride to the airport, flying is an everyday miracle of modern transport that will almost always prove your worst fears to be groundless. During 2000, for instance, there were a total of 36 fatal airliner accidents across the world, including nine involving jet airliners.

Given the enormous amount of international air traffic on any given day, that means your chances of being in a crash are less than 1 in 12 million. Which, admittedly, is still a chance.

There's no escaping the fact that aircraft do sometimes crash, whether through human error, metal fatigue, acts of nature, or acts of terror. Most accidents occur during the intricate phases of takeoff, climb, descent, and landing. The good news is that even in those cases, as many as 20 per cent of passengers survive.

Please fasten your seat belts and put your seats in the upright position. Your safety briefing is about to begin.

Listen to the Pre-Flight Safety Briefing.

No matter how many times you've had to sit through it, there is always something useful to be gleaned from the up-front pantomime. Bear in mind, too, that safety information, such as the location of emergency exits, may vary from plane to plane.

Be Prepared to Make a Quick Exit.

As soon as you board the plane, make a note of the number of rows between your seat and the nearest emergency exits. If you are sitting next to an emergency door, it's because the airline has judged you to be physically and mentally capable of opening it. But read the instructions anyway. You may have to make your escape through a plane wreathed in smoke and fire, so work out a way to do it in the dark. Base your plan of action on the fact that you will most probably have to get out on your own.

Avoid Synthetic Fibres.

Fire, smoke, and toxic gasses are the big killers in most aircraft crashes. You will increase your chances of survival if you wear comfortable, unrestrictive clothing in natural fabrics, such as cotton, wool, denim or leather. (You'll look better, too.) Synthetics, such as polyester or nylon, will melt in the flames and cling to your skin. Avoid sandals, in favour of lace-up shoes or boots. Cover your arms and legs as fully as possible.

Brace Yourself.

With your seat belt securely fastened, place a pillow or windbreaker on your lap. Put your head down. Cross your arms over your calves, and grab your ankles. Slide your feet forward. Close your eyes. And try not to panic.

Think About Buying a Personal Smoke Hood.

There have been many cases of rescuers breaking down the door of a plane, only to discover that the majority of passengers have died not from impact, but from the inhalation of toxic gasses. Smoke contains carbon monoxide and a host of other odourless, colourless chemicals that can kill in seconds. A personal smoke hood is a small device, packaged in a luminous canister, that allows you to breathe pure, filtered air for up to 20 minutes. Otherwise, cover your mouth and nose with a moistened handkerchief or headrest cover.

Listen to the pre-flight safety briefing.

HOW TO SURVIVE A FIRE IN YOUR CAR

You're cruising down the freeway at your customary speed, when you suddenly detect a faint whiff of burning in the air. Two possible reasons. One: you're driving too fast. Two: your car's on fire. Either way, it's time to slow down and take corrective action.

When you consider that cars are basically hulks of hot metal, glass and rubber, powered by one of the most flammable (not to mention inflammable) substances on earth, it's a miracle that more of them don't spontaneously combust on our roads.

Slow down when your car gets too hot to handle.

Certainly, no movie car chase worth its product placement ends without a sky-high explosion, but in the real world car fires are a lot less spectacular and a lot less frequent. Which is why they can really take you by surprise when they do happen.

Aside from collisions and "rollovers", the cause could be anything from an oil leak to an electrical fault to a Molotov Cocktail tossed through your window. Here's how to keep your cool when your car gets a little too hot to handle.

Pull Over, Switch Off, Get Out.

If you notice smoke or flames anywhere in your vehicle, don't try to drive to the nearest garage. Signal your intentions, and pull off the road as soon as it's safe. Switch off the engine, and get everyone out of the car. Disconnect the battery if you can. Warn oncoming traffic, and keep curious onlookers at bay. If it's a small fire, you might be able to fight it. If in any doubt, call the fire brigade.

Watch Out for Exploding Components.

The obvious and immediate danger in a car fire is that petrol vapours may ignite and explode the tank. But other parts of your car can also unexpectedly go BOOM. The tyres for example. And the shock absorbers. Some bumpers are also filled with a special kind of fluid, which could expand under pressure and send the bumper flying. In other words, don't stand too close to the car.

Pass the Fire-Extinguisher.

Although it's not a legal requirement in South Africa, it's a good idea to carry an easily accessible dry powder or BCF-type fire-extinguisher in your car. Both are effective at fighting electrical fires. The standard formula for using a fire-extinguisher is PASS: Pull the safety pin, Aim at the base of the flames, Squeeze the handle, and Sweep back and forth. If the flames are coming from under the bonnet, don't open it, or you'll give the fire the oxygen it needs to spread.

Pass the fire extinguisher.

Try to Smother the Flames.

If they're not yet raging out of control, and you don't have a fire-extinguisher to hand, you can try using a car rug, blanket, or any thick, non-synthetic material to smother the flames.

Watch Where You're Standing.

Never stand in fluids that are leaking from a burning car. Always stand upwind and far away from the flames and smoke, as the fabrics and materials of your car could give off toxic gasses.

HOW TO SURVIVE
A SINKING SHIP

Ever since Kate Winslet and Leonardo diCaprio clung to each other in the icy Atlantic in *Titanic*, millions of romantic souls have set out to revive the Golden Age of ocean travel, conveniently overlooking the fact that the lovers were only in the sea in the first place because their ship hit an iceberg.

Always keep a lookout for icebergs.

No modern liner would ever be described as unsinkable, which is why "Fire" and "Abandon Ship" drills are as much a feature of on-board life as quoits on deck and dinner at the Captain's Table.

Fortunately, today's commercial vessels are required to carry more than their full quota of life jackets and life craft, which will usually be equipped with everything from first-aid kits to sea anchors to catchment tubes for collecting drinkable rainwater. Shipboard communication and airborne rescue have also come a long way since the days when Kate and Leo went cruising.

So sit back, relax, enjoy the ride, and don't forget to take your seasickness tablets BEFORE you climb into the lifeboat.

Don't All Rush at Once.

If you hear the urgent series of bells, whistles and announcements that tell you to abandon ship for real, proceed quickly and calmly to the nearest muster station, where you will be equipped with a life jacket if you are not already wearing one. It can take anywhere from 15 minutes to a few hours for an ocean-going vessel to sink. Your chances of survival will increase dramatically if you follow instructions, remember your drills, and manage not to panic.

If You Have to Jump, Jump Feet First.

Ideally, you will be safely huddled in a lifeboat or life raft when you hit the waves. If you absolutely have to jump, get as close to the water as you can, put your legs together, keep your body straight, press your elbows to your sides, grip the top of your life jacket, look straight ahead … and jump. Your life jacket will maintain its buoyancy even it is punctured or torn, so you will quickly rise to the surface.

Get as close to the water as you can before jumping.

Put Your Knees Up and Relax.

Any unnecessary thrashing or movement in the water will lead to rapid heat loss, so don't try to swim ashore unless it's very close by. If you need to reach a life raft, a fellow survivor, or a floating piece of wreckage, swim slowly and deliberately to conserve your energy. Otherwise, remain as still as you can, with your elbows to your side and your arms wrapped tightly around your knees. This is known as the Heat Escape Lessening Posture, or HELP for short. If you have no other option, keep your head above water and hold your position until help arrives.

Dress as Warmly as You Can.

Whatever the weather on board, you can safely bet it's going to be freezing cold in the water. (Try to get shipwrecked in the Indian Ocean if you must; it's a few degrees warmer.) Your immediate priority will be to protect yourself against heat loss, which can lead to heart failure and hypothermia. Cover up from head to toe, with as many layers of clothing as you can. Just remember to leave a little room for your life jacket.

Huddle.

Whether you're in the water or on a life raft, now's the time to cast aside all distinctions of class and caste, and get as close to your fellow survivors as possible. In the water, float in small "scrums" with your arms around one another's shoulders for moral and physical support. On a raft, huddle close together, and share food, drinking water, energy, tasks and warmth. After all, you're all in the same boat.

6
THE CRIME WAVE

HOW TO SURVIVE A HIJACKING

Although you stand at least a small chance of being accosted and relieved of your vehicle in just about any major metropolis, hijacking has become the quintessential South African crime. As a dual-function act, it enables the perpetrator to steal a valuable piece of personal property, and at the same time provides the means for a speedy getaway.

The danger time for hijacking is between 4pm and 8pm on a weekday, especially a Friday, when traffic peaks earlier and drivers are more relaxed. Most hijackings last no more than two minutes. While some hijackers are armed with nothing more sophisticated than a rock or a wheel spanner, the threat of violence is almost always present.

Many hijackings are well planned and commissioned by syndicates, but you can just as easily be hijacked on impulse at a stop street, a filling station, or even a drive-in cinema. Be alert, be aware, and be sure you know how to make the right decision when it comes to your car or your life.

*Many hijackings are well planned and
commissioned by syndicates.*

Don't Brake for Hijackers.

Because it's easier to hijack a car when it's stationary, keep
your guard up at stop streets and traffic lights. This
doesn't give you an excuse to hit the petrol rather than
the brake – although the magistrate might buy your story
if you can come up with a convincing enough set of local
crime statistics – but it does mean you should be extra
observant when slowing to a halt, especially after dark.

Beware of Flying Spark Plugs.

The first clue that you're being hijacked may be the
shattering sound of your window giving in to a well-
practised swing from an expertly wielded spark plug.
Lessen the chances of a "smash and grab" by unwinding
your window very slightly, which will make it more
flexible and three times harder to break.

Give Yourself Room to Move.

Many hijackings take place in the driveway of your ultimate destination – home. Don't relax until you're right inside. You're particularly vulnerable while waiting for the automatic gate to open. Don't wait in front of the gate. Wait on the left-hand side of the road, with enough of a gap to prevent you from being boxed in. Always try to maximise the number of directions in which you can manoeuvre your car.

Leave the Keys in the Car.

If you have to get out of your car to open the gate, leave the keys in the ignition. Sure, they're an open invitation, but you'll avoid a direct confrontation with a hijacker lying in wait. Ignore this advice if you have children in the car: take the keys, which you may be able to use as a bargaining tool.

Don't Make Any Sudden Movements.

Hijacking is a desperate, dangerous way to make a living. Your hijacker may be a cool, hardened professional, or a wide-eyed bundle of nerves. Either way, don't take chances. Your car is just a dead piece of metal. Let it go. Keep your hands visible as you turn to get out of the car. Keep your right hand up. Use your left hand to engage the handbrake, put the car in neutral, and release your seat belt. Don't look the hijacker in the eyes. Don't do anything unexpected. Even an accidental blast on the hooter could be enough to trigger a tragic response.

Stay With Your Children.

Very few hijackings involve children being driven off in the car. A child in a car turns a hijacking into a high-priority crime with a nationwide alert. But just in case, shepherd your children out with great care, and don't get separated from them. Let a child in the passenger seat follow you out on the driver's side. Keep your child-seat behind the driver's seat, so that you'll be able to open the door and unbuckle your child as you get out. Use your car as a step to reach for your children, so that you'll stay with them if it suddenly takes off.

HOW TO SURVIVE A SHOOT-OUT

Cars may backfire, corks may pop, and firecrackers may explode, but of all the sounds that punctuate the South African landscape, none is quite as calculated to attract your attention as that of a gun fired in anger.

Indeed, even a gun fired in jubilation isn't that much fun to listen to. Since South Africa is one of the most heavily armed societies in the world, with a ratio of around 100 registered firearms per 1,000 people, chances are good that you'll hear that sound sooner or later.

The new Firearms Control Act, signed into law in 2000, makes it a lot harder for law-abiding citizens to own an arsenal of weapons, or to shoot first and fire warning shots later. We can safely assume, however, that not everyone who wields a firearm in public will be acting in accordance with the Act.

Here's how to take care of yourself when that shadowy object on someone's hip turns out not to be a cellular phone after all.

Reach for the Sky.

If you find yourself staring down the barrel of a gun, your best chance of survival is full compliance with whatever is demanded of you. Maintain a deadpan expression, make no sudden movements, and keep your hands where they can be seen. Don't look the gun-holder in the eye. Try not to scream or panic. Your assailant may be even more nervous than you are.

Get Level With the Gravel.

If you hear shooting around you, you're better off hitting the dirt than running wildly for cover. The shooter will most likely be shooting from the waist or higher, so belly-on-the-ground is the best place to be. If you're indoors, dive under the furniture, cover your head with your hands, and stay there until the smoke has cleared.

Hit the dirt, and keep your head down.

Roll for Cover if You Can.

If you're on the ground, and things are getting hairy, weigh up the prospect of attracting fire against the prospect of reaching cover with two or three quick rolls of your body. They don't teach this kind of movement in aerobics classes in South Africa. They should.

Hold your fire.

If you are opposed to gun control, your fellow citizens have every right to expect that you will know how to control your gun. And that means not returning fire in a public place, unless you are 100 per cent confident of your ability to do so without making things worse or hitting the wrong people.

Bite the Bullet.

Your big priority, if you've just been shot and you're conscious enough to do something about it, is to stop the bleeding in any way you can. Use a handkerchief or an item of clothing, and apply direct and constant pressure to the wound. There may be an exit as well as an entry wound, so expect a lot of blood.

They don't teach this kind of movement in aerobics classes in South Africa. They should.

HOW TO SURVIVE
A STREET ATTACK

You may live behind walls topped with electrified wire, in a house fitted with infrared sensors and closed circuit cameras. You may be guarded round the clock by pitbull terriers, and you may never even take a shower without a panic button round your neck. But sooner or later, like it or not, you're going to have to step out of your cocoon and deal with the challenge of life on the street.

Relax. A healthy dose of paranoia will serve you well in any urban environment, but it's a little unfair to suspect that EVERYONE is out to get you. (And if they are, it's probably not personal.) As long as you look like you belong, and you're wise enough not to wander where you don't belong, you'll generally be as safe in the big city as you are at home.

Here's what to do when your paranoia turns out to be justified.

Don't Look For Spare Change on the Pavement.

Sure, you'll probably find dozens of 1c pieces that no-one else can be bothered to pick up. But you'll also mark yourself, to any watching predators, as someone who is easily distracted and less than fully aware of their surroundings. Same applies if you're wearing headphones, or trying to read a map while walking. Don't look like a good victim. Stride confidently, with head held high, as if you know exactly where you're going.

Try to Shake Off Your Shadow.

If you suspect someone is following you (and not just because you look as if you know where you're going) try changing direction suddenly, crossing the street, or doubling your pace. If that doesn't work, stop in your tracks, turn around and loudly demand to know what your pursuer wants. Could be you just dropped your wallet a couple of blocks back.

Run For It.

Okay, so you are being mugged, and you do have a gun or knife pointing at you. Your three basic options: fight, flee, or hand over the money. If you choose to flee, do so at speed, and keep up the screaming and shouting. Run into a shop, an office block, anywhere that looks safer than the street. Become a moving target. Guns can only fire in a straight line, so be sure to follow a zig-zag path.

Fight Dirty.

It's usually not wise to argue with a gun or knife. But if you're being held in a tight grip, or if you're simply "mad as hell and not going to take it any more", fight back with any weapon and tactic at your disposal. Bite, kick, gouge, scratch, jab. Go for the sensitive bits: eyes, nose, ears, groin, windpipe. If you have anything sharp in your possession – a key, a comb, a pen – stab your assailant with all the force and fury you can muster. And keep screaming and shouting all the while.

Use Your Voice as a Weapon.

If you're convinced you're about to be mugged, and there are a lot of other people around, use your loudest scream or shout as a weapon of first resort. At the very least, you'll buy yourself time, and your would-be assailant will most likely back off and find someone quieter. Experts advise you should avoid shouting "help!" which usually has as much effect as a squealing car alarm in a busy urban setting. Shout "fire!" instead. Unless, of course, you've got a gun pointing at you.

Use your voice as a weapon.

7

DOMESTIC DRAMAS

HOW TO SURVIVE A FIRE IN YOUR HOME

It begins with a pan of chips left cooking on the stove; a curtain drifting too close to the bars of a glowing heater; a cigarette left smouldering on a couch or in a bed. Within minutes, every combustible in your house is combusting, and you're standing outside, dazed by the flames, trying to remember whether you got around to posting that premiums cheque to your insurance broker.

You can avoid this nightmare scenario by being "firewise": unplugging major electrical appliances when they're not in use; never leaving stoves and heaters unattended; keeping matches well out of reach of children; installing smoke alarms; banning indoor smoking in accordance with Government regulations; and knowing which of the five types of fire extinguisher – Water, Dry Powder, CO_2, Foam, and Halon or BCF – to use on which type of fire.

Failing all that, at least know how to get out of your house in a hurry, where your family should gather for roll call, and which cellular or land line emergency number will summon the screaming red engines in the shortest possible time. Here's what to do before they get there.

Never leave a hot stove unattended.

If You Can't Fight the Fire, Contain It.

Firefighting is a job for professionals. You may think you can handle a small blaze in the kitchen or lounge, but small blazes have a habit of very quickly turning into raging fires. If you don't have the skills and equipment to tame a fire, your priority should be to contain it. Shut doors and windows behind you as you make your way to safety. Conversely, if you're trying to escape from a burning house, don't open a door before testing the door knob with the back of your hand. If it's hot to the touch, try another route.

Stay Low, and Go.

Most victims of house fires succumb to smoke and toxic fumes, rather than to the flames themselves. Since hot air rises, your best bet is to drop to your hands and knees and crawl your way out, preferably with a wet handkerchief or cloth over your mouth and nose. Stay close to the walls, where the foundations of your house are at their strongest.

Stop, Drop, and Roll.

If your clothes catch fire, don't run. Instead, drop to the floor and roll slowly, over and over, to smother the flames. Cover your face with your hands. If you see someone else on fire, never use a fire extinguisher to put them out. The chemicals will only make things worse. Use water, or cover the victim with a blanket, curtains, or a rug. Ideally, get one of those space-age-style fire blankets when you next stock up with fire-extinguishers for your home.

Don't Jump! (Unless You Really Have To)

If you're stuck on an upper storey when a fire breaks out, get to a balcony or other safe point and await rescue. If you really have no other option, and you're not too high up, tie bed sheets or curtain ropes together in the classic escape style, and lower yourself carefully to the ground. Throw pillows or bedding to break your fall.

Don't Rush Back Into a Burning House to Call the Fire Brigade.

Call them first, or use the neighbour's phone. You shouldn't return to a burning house for any reason, which is why it's so important to have a pre-arranged meeting place where you can check that every family member and pet is present, safe and accounted for.

HOW TO SURVIVE BEING ATTACKED BY A SWARM OF BEES

Next to the drone of an electric lawn mower and the soft pukka-pukk of an automatic pool cleaner, there is no sound as evocative of a summer day as the buzzing of a honeybee flitting from flower to flower to the open mouth of your soft-drink can.

Aside from such minor irritations, bees are docile, preoccupied creatures that rarely sting without good reason, and even then, never more than once. While the African Honeybee is a more aggressive breed – the ancestor of the notorious "killer bees" that have sown panic across the southern states of America – you are still largely safe from attack if you do not disturb a hive or stand in the way of a migrating swarm.

Bee stings can be life-threatening to allergy-prone individuals, the elderly, people with a history of heart and chest complaints, and victims of multiple stings (more than 15 at a time). Here's the buzz on how to cope when bees go wild.

Don't Irritate the Bees.

Bees are hypersensitive to certain sounds and scents. Chain saws, lawn mowers, and weed-eaters – in fact, anything that makes a noise like a swarm of angry bees –

can anger and provoke an otherwise peaceful hive. You're also more likely to be attacked if you're wearing dark clothing, and certain floral or citrus perfumes. If you discover a hive on your property, call a team of professionals (look under Beekeepers in the Yellow Pages.) Never pour petrol over a hive, or otherwise try to deal with the problem yourself. You'll only get stung.

Buzz Off.

The best strategy for dealing with an attack by a swarm of angry bees is: run like crazy. (Preferably not in the direction of the hive.) Do not pause to swat the bees or throw things at them. Cover your face with your shirt or your arm – stings to the eyes, mouth, nose and throat can be deadly – and seek shelter as quickly as you can. Shut all doors and windows, and wait until the bees have dispersed. If you're outdoors, run through tall scrub or bush, which will confuse and slow the swarm.

Run like crazy.

Don't Dive Into a Pool.

Bees aren't that easily fooled. They'll hover in formation overhead, and renew their attack as soon as you come up for air.

Reach For Your Knife or Credit Card.

The thought that a bee gave its life to sting you may be of small comfort as you try to get to grips with the resulting pain. You need to get the stingers out as soon as possible, and you need to get them out the right way. Do not squeeze or use tweezers. You'll only spread more venom into the wound. Instead, use a dull blade, a credit card, or the edge of a fingernail to scrape the stinger away. Wash the affected area with soap and water, and apply an ice pack if necessary.

Watch Out for the Danger Signs.

In most cases, a bee sting will cause nothing more than mild irritation and swelling. Seek medical help immediately if you have difficulty breathing, if your face is swelling, or if you feel generally weak and sick. If you've been stung 15 times or more, you could also be in danger of further complications. The average adult can tolerate more than 1,000 stings in one go, but quick treatment is essential.

HOW TO SURVIVE A DOG ATTACK

Bred over centuries for loyalty, protection and companionship, dogs are the world's most intelligent species, next to cats, dolphins and people. (Okay, some people.)

All this will be small comfort should you find yourself in a face-off with an animal that can't even tell the difference between a bona fide criminal and someone who just wants to enjoy a nice, quiet stroll around the neighbourhood.

Most dogs are content to bark in defence of their territorial imperative; others are hard-wired to snarl, bare their teeth, raise the hackles on their backs, and go straight for the jugular. The following tactics may come in handy when a simple "voetsak" fails to do the trick.

Learn to Read a Dog's Mind.

Not too many generations back, dogs were wild wolves roaming the steppes of Siberia. That genetic memory lies just below the surface of today's domesticated breeds, as you'll discover when you encounter a dog getting ready to defend its territory. Learn to read the nuances of posture and movement that accompany displays of aggression, fear and uncertainty. Just because a dog is wagging its tail doesn't necessarily mean it's happy to see you.

Stand Your Ground.

In a conventional conflict situation, your basic option is fight or flight. When it's you versus a dog, your safest bet is to follow the middle path. In other words, STAY PUT. Do not look the dog in the eye. Do not raise your hands. Do not make any sudden movements. Allow yourself to be sniffed, and if necessary licked. If you're lucky, the dog will go away, and leave you free to jog another day.

Try Dodging Out of the Way at the Last Second.

A charging dog relies on its momentum to knock you to the ground. At which point, you're dog food. Avoid this prospect, if you can, by standing close to a tree, wall or other obstacle, and then moving behind it at the last second. The dog will be forced to slow down and "re-group", giving you precious time to get up the tree or over the wall.

Don't Put Up a Fight (Unless it's a Small Dog).

For the sake of human dignity alone, the "stand-and-be-sniffed rule" can safely be ignored if your attacker is a small, yapping dog of the ornamental variety. In this case, feel free to shout, charge, and – if it's a Maltese

Poodle – kick until the nuisance goes away. Bear in mind, however, that South African household dogs often hang out in pairs, and the other half may well be a Rottweiler or German Shepherd.

Be aware that South African household dogs often hang out in pairs.

Shove Your Hand All the Way Down the Dog's Throat.

When all else fails, and you find yourself in the line of attack of a killer dog with wide-open jaws, the last thing you should do is turn tail and run. That's just the kind of light exercise killer dogs like. Instead, try the disarmingly simple technique of shoving your hand as far as it will go down the dog's throat. The dog will gag, and you will almost certainly get your arm back.

Offer the Dog a Well-Padded Arm.

As seen in countless dog shows and charity displays by the South African Police Services. In the absence of a large roll of hessian, wrap whatever clothing or material you can around your arm, and let the dog have it. Use your free hand to fight back, preferably with a rock or a stick.

Wrap whatever clothing or material you can around your arm.

How to Survive
Your Medical Aid
(The Discovery Health Way)

By Harry Dugmore

If there is an art to survival, it is the art of being prepared. It is the art of taking stock of any given situation, and arming yourself with the skills and know-how to deal with whatever life might throw at you. That means taking a map and compass with you when you head into the Great Outdoors, or a flashlight when you go camping. It also means making sure that you have a Health Plan that works for you.

Indeed, if *Madam & Eve's South African Survival Handbook* had been published 10 years ago, the biggest question might have been: how can you survive your Medical Aid Scheme?

By the late 1980s, medical aids were slow-moving institutions that people loved to hate. Costs shot up each year as fast as customer service levels fell. In the early part of 1992, a radically different way of financing health needs was invented, by a then tiny company called Momentum Health. Discovery, the presenters of this book, unveiled ideas that were so different that they immediately changed the rules of the game.

From the beginning, Discovery's early pioneers, led by Adrian Gore and Barry Swartzberg, focussed on three areas of great concern to users of traditional medical schemes: costs, service levels and customer well-being.

In terms of costs, Discovery's early plans focussed on trying to bring down the overall costs of health cover by offering clients a hybrid of insurance-based medical cover, and a personal "savings account", in one product. The savings account would accumulate funds that could be used for the "runny noses and dentist bills" – the relatively small but regular amounts needed to keep a family healthy – while an insurance component would be used for more unpredictable, catastrophic health needs.

This core idea was both radical and yet easy to understand. With individual risk properly rated and users taking some responsibility for their own health spending, Discovery could offer longer-term benefits and financial stability in an otherwise unstable industry. The new plan transformed members from passive recipients of medical aid into active partners in their own health. Adrian Gore says, "Getting people involved in their own health care, making them partners in keeping costs down, in staying healthy, was the basis from which we built."

In addition to new ways of rating risk and apportioning cost, Discovery also took a different view of how to communicate with customers, providing them with the tools they needed to participate confidently in their own health plans. "Right from the start, we wanted to work exclusively through brokers – well-informed intermediaries who could really look after our customers," says Neville Koopowitz, Marketing Director.

Medical schemes had tended not to use brokers up to then, and few people actually understood what their medical schemes did and didn't do. Discovery extended the ideas of providing highly trained intermediaries with a different approach to the brokers themselves. "I started with an attitude that the guys in the front line are the rainmakers, and we are there to support them," says Gore.

The third area where Discovery wanted to do things differently was in customer service, traditionally an area where medical aid schemes were appalling. In those days, clients often waited months for repayments and everyone had a medical aid service horror story to tell.

"When we started off, we looked at credit card companies for an example of how things could be done', Adrian says. "You paid for something, it got debited almost immediately from your account, with a minimum of fuss and hassle for you. We wanted to reduce our clients' payment claim times radically, and dazzle our customers with high-touch service. We thought if we could do that well, customers would come to us."

So committed was Discovery to introducing new levels of service, the company did not initially hire staff who had previously worked for medical aid schemes.

Armed with these unconventional views, and serious support from Rand Merchant Bank, Discovery was ready by 1993 to unveil its product range and receive its first clients. But it wasn't easy. Barry Swartzberg remembers: "We had to convince the staff at RMB, almost one by one. Eventually, they voted, and we were in. But outside of that, we just didn't have the business. Despite all our planning, we were like the local under-10 soccer side.

Everyone did everything. I remember when we got the RMB account, all of us sat around one afternoon, including Adrian and me, cutting and pasting the membership cards."

Despite the slow start, due largely to the radical nature of their new health plan, Discovery eventually got their first independent client, a small motor company called Orbit. This was followed by their first big client, a division of Nashua. "There was this legendary broker who was selling our product for us," says Swartzberg. "One day he walked in and said, 'I've just signed Nashua'. We were bowled over. It was April 1993, and we'd all been out there, especially Adrian, selling, networking, and all of a sudden Nashua arrived. It just changed the business."

Discovery was able to double their membership every year for their first five years. By 2001, the company covered over a million lives.

Part of the reason for the rapid growth is Discovery's responsiveness to market conditions. Discovery's core product offering has been changed and refined almost every year, and often more than once a year, in response to the changing customer needs and new regulatory environments.

Changes in the law have in fact been one of the company's biggest challenges. From early 2000, the government asked all the so-called new generation schemes, pioneered by Discovery, to eliminate individual risk rating from the way they allowed people to join the schemes. And, at the same time, the government restricted the basis on which companies could decline new members, even if they had pre-existing illnesses.

Some other companies in the health-plan business went into a tail spin. Discovery knuckled down and reworked its product offering over and over again, eventually winning approval for their new product structures – and more and more customers. "What could have sunk us, strengthened us," says Gore.

A large part of what makes Discovery different is the emphasis it places on wellness. Right from the start, the founders asked: what if Discovery could reward its members for exercising more, giving up smoking, and for getting tested regularly for cholesterol and conditions? And what if the company made it easier for people to reduce the stresses in their lives by encouraging rest and relaxation, partly through unprecedented rates for flying and staying at hotels?

The answer was establishment of the Vitality programme, the results of which have transformed Discovery. Never before had a company stood so clearly for the well-being of its customers. For example, in 2000, almost 300 members a day took advantage of air fares and holiday hotel stays at unprecedented rates. Discovery members had 250,000 gym work-outs in 2000, while almost 10,000 gave up smoking and 21 000 Run/Walk For Life training sessions were purchased. Discovery also encouraged 55,000 dental checks, 84,000 pap smears and 65,000 cholesterol screens during the same period.

By putting an emphasis on staying healthy, Discovery ensures that members incur fewer medical bills. And the way the Vitality programme has been run delights customers, who love the value-for-money flights, gym memberships and medical tests. "It's a classic win-win situation," says Neville Koopowitz, "our members stay healthier, and we can ensure that if and when they do get sick, they get the best medical treatment available."

Swartzberg sums up what makes Discovery different: "Our philosophy is that when you're sick, we cover you completely. If you're healthy we're going to encourage you to stay healthy."

Adds Gore: "As we had envisioned in the beginning, we want to do all of this with levels of customer service not usually seen in either the medical aid or insurance industry. We try to create products that people aspire to purchase. And then, once they become part of the 'Discovery Community', we work hard to impress them – either when they use our products, or when they have contact with our company in any way."

These values and skills have allowed it to launch Destiny Health in the USA in 2000, and introduce a wide variety of new services to its clients back in South Africa. Discovery Life now offers life assurance products based on very different principles from those of its competitors. Going forward, Discovery will continue to enhance Vitality and its core products.

Gore sums up: "Our vision is to make people healthier, and enhance and protect lifestyles. With the enthusiasm and dedication of the people at Discovery, and the belief we all have in this vision, I believe we can build a truly great company that never stops innovating."